COACHING YOUTH

BASKETBALL

SECOND EDITION

American Sport Education Program

Human Kinetics

Library of Congress Cataloging-in-Publication Data

Coaching youth basketball / American Sport Education Program. -- 2nd ed.
    p. cm.
  Rev. ed. of: Rookie coaches basketball guide. c1991.
  ISBN 0-87322-892-8 (paper)
  1. Basketball--Coaching. I. American Sport Education Program.
  II. Rookie coaches basketball guide.
  GV885.3.C63 1995   95-14388
  796.323'07'7--dc20   CIP

ISBN: 0-87322-892-8

Coaching Youth Basketball is the second edition of *Rookie Coaches Basketball Guide*.

Acquisitions Editor: Jim Kestner; **Basketball Consultant:** Kelly Hill; **Developmental Editor:** Jan Colarusso Seeley; **Assistant Editor:** Erin Cler; **Editorial Assistant:** Andrew Starr; **Copyeditor:** Karen Bojda; **Proofreader:** Dena Popara; **Graphic Artist:** Francine Hamerski; **Text Designer:** Judy Henderson; **Cover Designer:** Stuart Cartwright; **Photographer (cover):** John Kilroy; **Interior Art:** Tim Stiles, cartoons; Paul To, line drawings; and Studio 2D, Mac art; **Printer:** United Graphics

Copies of this book are available at special discounts for bulk purchase for sales promotions, premiums, fund-raising, or educational use. Special editions or book excerpts can also be created to specifications. For details, contact the Special Sales Manager at Human Kinetics.

Printed in the United States of America   10 9 8 7 6 5 4

Human Kinetics
Web site: http://www.humankinetics.com/

United States: Human Kinetics, P.O. Box 5076, Champaign, IL 61825-5076
1-800-747-4457
e-mail: humank@hkusa.com

Canada: Human Kinetics, Box 24040, Windsor, ON N8Y 4Y9
1-800-465-7301 (in Canada only)
e-mail: humank@hkcanada.com

Europe: Human Kinetics, P.O. Box IW14, Leeds LS16 6TR, United Kingdom
(44) 1132 781708
e-mail: humank@hkeurope.com

Australia: Human Kinetics, 57A Price Avenue, Lower Mitcham, South Australia 5062
(088) 277 1555
e-mail: humank@hkaustralia.com

New Zealand: Human Kinetics, P.O. Box 105-231, Auckland 1
(09) 523 3462
e-mail: humank@hknewz.com

Contents

Welcome to Coaching!

Coaching young people is an exciting way to be involved in sport. But it isn't easy. The untrained novice coach may be overwhelmed by the responsibilities involved in helping athletes through their early sport experiences. Preparing youngsters physically and mentally in their sport and providing them with a positive role model are among the difficult—but rewarding—tasks you will assume as a coach.

This book will help you meet the challenges and experience the rewards of coaching young athletes. We call it *Coaching Youth Basketball* because it is intended for coaches who are working with developing basketball players. In this book you'll learn how to apply general coaching principles and teach basketball rules, skills, and strategies successfully to kids. This book also serves as a text for the American Sport Education Program's (ASEP) Rookie Coaches Course.

We hope you will find coaching rewarding and that you will continue to learn more about coaching and your sport so that you can be the best possible coach for your young athletes.

If you would like more information about ASEP and its Rookie Coaches Course, please contact us at

ASEP
P.O. Box 5076
Champaign, IL 61825-5076
1-800-747-5698

Good Coaching!

Unit 1

Who, Me . . . a Coach?

If you are like most rookie coaches, you have probably been recruited from the ranks of concerned parents, sport enthusiasts, or community volunteers. And, like many rookie and veteran coaches, you probably have had little formal instruction on how to coach. But when the call went out for coaches to assist with the local youth basketball program, you answered because you like children and enjoy basketball, and perhaps because you want to be involved in a worthwhile community activity.

I Want to Help, but . . .

Your initial coaching assignment may be difficult. Like many volunteers, you may not know much about the sport you have agreed to coach or about how to work with children between the ages of 6 and 14. Relax, because *Coaching Youth Basketball* will help you find the answers to such common questions as these:

- What do I need to be a good coach?
- How can I best communicate with my players?
- How do I go about teaching sport skills?
- What can I do to promote safety?
- What should I do when someone is injured?
- What are the basic rules, skills, and strategies of basketball?
- What practice drills will improve my players' basketball skills?

Before answering these questions, let's take a look at what's involved in being a coach.

Am I a Parent or a Coach?

Many coaches are parents, but the two roles should not be confused. Unlike your role as a parent, as a coach you are responsible not only to yourself and your child, but also to the organization, all the players on the team (including your child), and their parents. Because of this additional responsibility, your behavior on the playing field will be different from your behavior at home, and your son or daughter may not understand why.

For example, imagine the confusion of a young boy who is the center of his parents' attention at home but is barely noticed by his father/coach in the sport setting. Or consider the mixed signals received by a young girl whose basketball skill is constantly evaluated by a mother/coach who otherwise rarely comments on her daughter's activities. You need to explain to your son or daughter your new responsibilities and how they will affect your relationship when coaching.

Take the following steps to avoid such problems in coaching your child:

- Ask your child if he or she wants you to coach the team.
- Explain why you wish to be involved with the team.
- Discuss how your interactions will change when you take on the role of coach at practice or games.
- Limit your coaching behavior to when you are in the coaching role.
- Avoid parenting during practice or game situations, to keep your role clear in your child's mind.
- Reaffirm your love for your child, irrespective of his or her performance on the basketball court.

What Are My Responsibilities as a Coach?

A coach assumes the responsibility of doing everything possible to ensure that the youngsters on his or her team will have an enjoyable and safe sporting experience while they learn sport skills.

Provide an Enjoyable Experience

Sport should be fun. Even if nothing else is accomplished, make certain your players have fun. Take the fun out of sport and you'll take the kids out of sport.

Children enter sport for a number of reasons (e.g., to meet and play with other children, to develop physically, and to learn skills), but their major objective is to have fun. Help them satisfy this goal by injecting humor and variety into your practices. Also, make games nonthreatening, festive experiences for your players. Such an approach will increase your players' desire to participate in the future, which should be the biggest goal of youth sport. Unit 2 will help you learn how to satisfy your players' yearning for fun and keep winning in perspective. And unit 3 will describe how you can effectively communicate this perspective to them.

Provide a Safe Experience

You are responsible for planning and teaching activities in such a way that the progression between activities minimizes risks (see units 4 and 5). Further, you must ensure that the facility at which your team practices and plays, and the equipment team members use, are free of hazards. Finally, you need to protect yourself from any legal liability that might arise from your involvement as a coach. Unit 5 will help you take the appropriate precautions.

Provide Opportunities for Children With Disabilities

There's a possibility that a child with a disability of some kind will register for your team. Don't panic! Your youth sport administrator or a number of organizations (see Appendix C) can provide you with information to help you best meet this child's needs.

As a coach, you need to know about the Americans with Disabilities Act (ADA). Passed in 1990, the ADA gives individuals the same legal protection against discrimination on the basis of disabilities as is provided against discrimination on the basis of race, gender, and class. The law does recognize that there are times when including an individual who is disabled might risk the safety of that individual and other players, but the exact way that courts are treating the ADA is still being decided. In general, the law requires that "reasonable accommodations" be made to include children with disabilities into organized sport programs. If a parent or child approaches you on the subject, and you aren't sure what to do, talk to the director in charge of your basketball program. If you make any decision on your own pertaining to the ADA, you may be vulnerable to a lawsuit.

Keep in mind that these children want to participate alongside their able-bodied peers. Give them the same support and encouragement that you give other athletes, and model their inclusion and acceptance for all your athletes.

Teach Basic Basketball Skills

In becoming a coach, you take on the role of educator. You must teach your players the fundamental skills and strategies necessary for success in their sport. That means that you need to "go to school."

If you don't know the basics of basketball now, you can learn them by reading the second half of this manual, units 6, 7, and 8. But even if you know basketball as a player, do you know how to teach it? This book will help you get started. There are also many valuable basketball books on the market, including those offered by Human Kinetics. See the ad in the back of this book or call 1-800-747-4457 for more information.

You'll also find it easier to provide good educational experiences for your players if you plan your practices. Unit 4 of this manual provides some guidelines for the planning process.

Getting Help

Veteran coaches in your league are an especially good source of help for you. They have all experienced the same emotions and concerns you are facing, and their advice can be invaluable as you work through your first season.

You can get additional help by watching basketball coaches in practices and games, attending workshops, reading basketball publications, and studying instructional videos. In addition to the American Sport Education Program (ASEP), the following national organizations will assist you in obtaining more basketball coaching information:

National Association of Basketball Coaches
9300 W. 110th St.
Suite 640
Overland Park, KS 66210
(913) 469-1001

USA Basketball
5465 Mark Dabling Blvd.
Colorado Springs, CO 80918
(719) 590-4800

Women's Basketball Coaches Association
4646 B Lawrenceville Hwy.
Lilburn, GA 30247
(404) 279-8027

Youth Basketball of America
P.O. Box 3067
Orlando, FL 32802-3067
(407) 363-9262

Amateur Athletic Union
3400 W. 86th St.
P.O. Box 68207
Indianapolis, IN 46268
(317) 872-2900

Coaching basketball is a rewarding experience. And your players will be rewarded if you learn all you can about coaching so you can be the best basketball coach you can be.

Unit 2

What Tools Do I Need as a Coach?

Have you purchased the traditional coaching tools—things like whistles, coaching clothes, sport shoes, and a clipboard? They'll help you coach, but to be a successful coach you'll need five other tools that cannot be bought. These tools are available only through self-examination and hard work; they're easy to remember using the acronym COACH:

C—Comprehension

O—Outlook

A—Affection

C—Character

H—Humor

Comprehension

Comprehension of the rules, skills, and tactics of basketball is required. It is essential that you understand the basic elements of the sport. To assist you in learning about the game, the second half of this guide describes rules, skills, and tactics and suggests how to plan for the season and individual practices. In the basketball-specific section of this guide, you'll also find a variety of drills to use in developing basketball skills.

To improve your comprehension of basketball, take the following steps:

- Read the sport-specific section of this book.
- Consider reading other basketball coaching books, including those available from ASEP (see pages 142 and 143 to order).
- Contact any of the organizations listed on page 7.
- Attend basketball clinics.
- Talk with other, more experienced, coaches.
- Observe local college, high school, and youth basketball games.
- Watch basketball games on television.

In addition to having basketball knowledge, you must implement proper training and safety methods so your players can participate with little risk of injury. Even then, sport injuries will occur. And more often than not, you'll be the first person responding to your players' injuries, so be sure you understand the basic emergency care procedures described in unit 5. Also, read in that unit how to handle more serious sport injury situations.

Outlook

This coaching tool refers to your perspective and goals—what you are seeking as a coach. The most common coaching objectives are (a) to have fun, (b) to help players develop their physical, mental, and social skills, and (c) to win. Thus your *outlook* involves the priorities you set, your planning, and your vision for the season.

To work successfully with children in a sport setting, you must have your priorities in order. In just what order do you rank the importance of fun, development, and winning?

Answer the following questions to examine your objectives:

Of which situation would you be most proud?

    a. Knowing that each participant enjoyed playing basketball.
    b. Seeing that all players improved their basketball skills.
    c. Winning the league championship.

Which statement best reflects your thoughts about sport?

    a. If it isn't fun, don't do it.

    b. Everyone should learn something every day.

    c. Sports aren't fun if you don't win.

How would you like your players to remember you?

    a. As a coach who was fun to play for.

    b. As a coach who provided a good base of fundamental skills.

    c. As a coach who had a winning record.

Which would you most like to hear a parent of a child on your team say?

    a. Billy really had a good time playing basketball this year.

    b. Susie learned some important lessons playing basketball this year.

    c. Jose played on the first-place basketball team this year.

Which of the following would be the most rewarding moment of your season?

    a. Having your team not want to stop playing, even after practice is over.

    b. Seeing one of your players finally master the skill of dribbling without constantly looking at the ball.

    c. Winning the league championship.

Look over your answers. If you most often selected "a" responses, then having fun is most important to you. A majority of "b" answers suggests that skill development is what attracts you to coaching. And if "c" was your most frequent response, winning is tops on your list of coaching priorities.

Most coaches say fun and development are more important, but when actually coaching, some coaches emphasize—indeed, overemphasize—winning. You, too, will face situations that challenge you to keep winning in its proper perspective. During such moments, you'll have to choose between emphasizing your players' development or winning. If your priorities are in order, your players' well-being will take precedence over your team's win-loss record every time.

Take the following actions to better define your outlook:

1. Determine your priorities for the season.

2. Prepare for situations that challenge your priorities.

3. Set goals for yourself and your players that are consistent with those priorities.

4. Plan how you and your players can best attain those goals.

5. Review your goals frequently to be sure that you are staying on track.

It is particularly important for coaches to permit all young athletes to participate. Each youngster—male or female, small or tall, gifted or disabled—should have an opportunity to develop skills and have fun.

Remember that the challenge and joy of sport is experienced through striving to win, not through winning itself. Players who aren't allowed off the bench are denied the opportunity to strive to win. And herein lies the irony: Coaches who allow all of their players to participate and develop skills will—in the end—come out on top.

ASEP has a motto that will help you keep your outlook in the best interest of the kids on your team. It summarizes in four words all you need to remember when establishing your coaching priorities:

Athletes First,
Winning Second

This motto recognizes that striving to win is an important, even vital, part of sport. But it emphatically states that no efforts in striving to win should be made at the expense of the athletes' well-being, development, and enjoyment.

Affection

Affection is another vital tool you will want to have in your coaching kit: a genuine concern for the young people you coach. It involves having a love for children, a desire to share with them your love and knowledge of basketball, and the patience and understanding that allow each individual playing for you to grow from his or her involvement in sport.

Successful coaches have a real concern for the health and welfare of their players. They care that each child on the team has an enjoyable and successful experience. They recognize that there are similarities between young people's sport experiences and other activities in their lives, and they encourage their players to strive to learn from all their experiences, to become well-rounded individuals. These coaches have a strong desire to work with children and be involved in their growth. And they have the patience to work with those who are slower to learn or less capable of performing. If you have such qualities or are willing to work hard to develop them, then you have the affection necessary to coach young athletes.

There are many ways to demonstrate your affection and patience, including these:

- Make an effort to get to know each player on your team.

- Treat each player as an individual.

- Empathize with players trying to learn new and difficult sport skills.
- Treat players as you would like to be treated under similar circumstances.
- Be in control of your emotions.
- Show your enthusiasm for being involved with your team.
- Keep an upbeat and positive tone in all of your communications.

Some children appreciate a pat on the back or shoulder as a sign of your approval or affection. But be aware that not all players feel comfortable with being touched. When this is the case, you need to respect their wishes.

Character

Character is a word that adults use frequently in conversations about sport experiences and young people. If you haven't already, you may one day be asked to explain whether you think sport builds good character. What will you say?

The fact that you have decided to coach young basketball players probably means that you think participation in sport is important. But whether or not that participation develops character in your players depends as much on you as it does the sport itself. How can you build character in your players?

Youngsters learn by listening to what adults say. But they learn even more by watching the behavior of certain important individuals. As a coach, you are likely to be a significant figure in the lives of your players. Will you be a good role model?

Having good character means modeling appropriate behaviors for sport and life. That means more than just saying the right things. What you say and what you do must match. There is no place in coaching for the "Do as I say, not as I do" philosophy. Challenge, support, encourage, and reward every child, and your players will be more likely to accept, even celebrate, their differences. Be in control before, during, and after all games and practices. And don't be afraid to admit that you were wrong. No one is perfect!

Many of us have been coached by someone who believes that criticizing players is a good way to build character. In reality, this approach damages children's self-esteem and teaches them that their value as a person is based on how they perform in sport. Unit 3 will help you communicate with your players in a way that builds positive self-esteem and develops your athletes' skills.

Finally, take stock of your own attitudes about ethnic, gender, and other stereotypes. You are an individual coach, and it would be wrong for others to form beliefs about you based on their personal attitudes about coaches in general. Similarly, you need to avoid making comments that support stereotypes of others. Let your words and actions show your players that every individual matters, and you will be teaching them a valuable lesson about respecting and supporting individuals' differences.

Consider the following steps to being a good role model:

- Take stock of your strengths and weaknesses.

- Build on your strengths.

- Set goals for yourself to improve upon those areas you would not like to see mimicked.

- If you slip up, apologize to your team and to yourself. You'll do better next time.

Humor

Humor is an often-overlooked coaching tool. For our use it means having the ability to laugh at yourself and with your players during practices and games. Nothing helps balance the tone of a serious, skill-learning session like a chuckle or two. And a sense of humor puts in perspective the many mistakes your young players will make. So don't get upset over each miscue or respond negatively to erring players. Allow your players and yourself to enjoy the ups, and don't dwell on the downs.

Here are some tips for injecting humor into your practices:

- Make practices fun by including a variety of activities.
- Keep all players involved in drills and scrimmages.
- Consider laughter by your players a sign of enjoyment, not waning discipline.
- Smile!

Where Do You Stand?

To take stock of your "coaching tool kit," rank yourself on the three questions for each of the five coaching tools. Simply circle the number that best describes your current status on each item.

Not at all		Somewhat		Very much so
1	**2**	**3**	**4**	**5**

Comprehension _____

1. Could you explain the rules of basketball to other parents without studying for a long time?

   1 2 3 4 5

2. Do you know how to organize and conduct safe basketball practices?

   1 2 3 4 5

3. Do you know how to provide first aid for most common, minor sport injuries?

   1 2 3 4 5

Comprehension Score: _____

Outlook

4. Do you place the interests of all children ahead of winning when you coach?   1 2 3 4 5
5. Do you plan for every meeting and practice?   1 2 3 4 5
6. Do you have a vision of what you want your players to be able to do by the end of the season?   1 2 3 4 5

Outlook Score: _____

Affection

7. Do you enjoy working with children?   1 2 3 4 5
8. Are you patient with youngsters learning new skills?   1 2 3 4 5
9. Are you able to show your players that you care?   1 2 3 4 5

Affection Score: _____

Character

10. Are your words and behaviors consistent with each other?   1 2 3 4 5
11. Are you a good model for your players?   1 2 3 4 5
12. Do you keep negative emotions under control before, during, and after games?   1 2 3 4 5

Character Score: _____

Humor

13. Do you usually smile at your players?   1 2 3 4 5
14. Are your practices fun?   1 2 3 4 5
15. Are you able to laugh at your mistakes?   1 2 3 4 5

Humor Score: _____

If you scored 9 or less on any of the coaching tools, be sure to reread those sections carefully. And even if you scored 15 on each tool, don't be complacent. Keep learning! Then you'll be well-equipped with the tools you need to coach young athletes.

Unit 3

How Should I Communicate With My Players?

Now you know the tools needed to COACH: Comprehension, Outlook, Affection, Character, and Humor. These are essentials for effective coaching; without them, you'd have a difficult time getting started. But none of those tools will work if you don't know how to use them with your athletes—and this requires skillful communication. This unit examines what communication is and how you can become a more effective communicator-coach.

What's Involved in Communication?

Coaches often mistakenly believe that communication involves only instructing players to do something, but verbal commands are a very small part of the communication process. More than half of what is communicated is nonverbal. So remember when you are coaching: Actions speak louder than words.

Communication in its simplest form involves two people: a sender and a receiver. The sender transmits the message verbally, through facial expression, and possibly through body language. Once the message is sent, the receiver must assimilate it successfully. A receiver who fails to attend or listen will miss parts, if not all, of the message.

How Can I Send More Effective Messages?

Young athletes often have little understanding of the rules and skills of basketball and probably even less confidence in playing it. So they need accurate, understandable, and supportive messages to help them along. That's why your verbal and nonverbal messages are so important.

Verbal Messages

"Sticks and stones may break my bones, but words will never hurt me" isn't true. Spoken words can have a strong and long-lasting effect. And coaches' words are particularly influential because youngsters place great importance on what coaches say. Perhaps you, like many former youth sport participants, have a difficult time remembering much of anything you were told by your elementary school teachers but can still recall several specific things your coaches at that level said to you. Such is the lasting effect of a coach's comments to a player.

Whether you are correcting misbehavior, teaching a player how to shoot the ball, or praising a player for good effort, there are a number of things you should consider when sending a message verbally. They include the following:

- *Be positive and honest.*
- *State it clearly and simply.*
- *Say it loud enough, and say it again.*
- *Be consistent.*

Be Positive and Honest

Nothing turns people off like hearing someone nag all the time, and young athletes react similarly to a coach who gripes constantly. Kids particularly need encouragement because they often doubt their abilities to perform in sport. So look for and tell your players what they did well.

But don't cover up poor or incorrect play with rosy words of praise. Kids know all too well when they've erred, and no cheerfully expressed cliché can undo their mistakes. If you fail to acknowledge players' errors, your athletes will think you are a phony.

State It Clearly and Simply

Positive and honest messages are good, but only if expressed directly in words your players understand. "Beating around the bush" is ineffective and inefficient. And if you do ramble, your players will miss the point of your message and probably lose interest. Here are some tips for saying things clearly:

- Organize your thoughts before speaking to your athletes.
- Explain things thoroughly, but don't bore them with long-winded monologues.

- Use language your players can understand. However, avoid trying to be hip by using their age group's slang vocabulary.

COMPLIMENT SANDWICH

A good way to handle situations in which you have identified and must correct improper technique is to serve your players a "compliment sandwich":

1. Point out what the athlete did correctly.
2. Let the player know what was incorrect in the performance and instruct him or her how to correct it.
3. Encourage the player by reemphasizing what he or she did well.

Say It Loud Enough, and Say It Again

Talk to your team in a voice that all members can hear and interpret. A crisp, vigorous voice commands attention and respect; garbled and weak speech is tuned out. It's OK, in fact, appropriate, to soften your voice when speaking to a player individually about a personal problem. But most of the time your messages will be for all your players to hear, so make sure they can! An enthusiastic voice also motivates players and tells them you enjoy being their coach. A word of caution, however: Don't dominate the setting with a booming voice that distracts attention from players' performances.

Sometimes what you say, even if stated loud and clear, won't sink in the first time. This may be particularly true with young athletes hearing words they don't understand. To avoid boring repetition and yet still get your message across, say the same thing in a slightly different way. For instance, you might first tell your players, "Guard your opponent at a safe distance." Soon afterward, remind them to "Make sure the opponent you are guarding cannot dribble around you for an easy basket." The second form of the message may get through to players who missed it the first time around.

Be Consistent

People often say things in ways that imply a different message. For example, a touch of sarcasm added to the words "way to go" sends an entirely different message than the words themselves suggest. It is essential that you avoid sending such mixed messages. Keep the tone of your voice consistent with the words you use. And don't say something one day and contradict it the next; players will get their wires crossed.

Nonverbal Messages

Just as you should be consistent in the tone of voice and words you use, you should also keep your verbal and nonverbal messages consistent. An extreme example of failing to do this would be shaking your head, indicating disapproval, while at the same time telling a player "Nice try." Which is the player to believe, your gesture or your words?

Messages can be sent nonverbally in a number of ways. Facial expressions and body language are just two of the more obvious forms of nonverbal signals that can help you when you coach.

Facial Expressions

The look on a person's face is the quickest clue to what he or she thinks or feels. Your players know this, so they will study your face, looking for any sign that will tell them more than the words you say. Don't try to fool them by putting on a happy or blank "mask." They'll see through it, and you'll lose credibility.

Serious, stone-faced expressions are no help to kids who need cues as to how they are performing. They will just assume you're unhappy or disinterested. Don't be afraid to smile. A smile from a coach can give a great boost to an unsure young athlete. Plus, a smile lets your players know that you are happy coaching them. But don't overdo it, or your players won't be able to tell when you are genuinely pleased by something they've done or when you are just putting on a smiling face.

Body Language

What would your players think you were feeling if you came to practice slouched over, with head down and shoulders slumped? Tired? Bored? Unhappy? What would they think you were feeling if you watched them during a contest with your hands on your hips, your jaws clenched, and your face reddened? Upset with them? Disgusted at an official? Mad at a fan? Probably some or all of these things would enter your players' minds. And none of these impressions is the kind you want your players to have of you. That's why you should carry yourself in a pleasant, confident, and vigorous manner. Such a posture not only projects happiness with your coaching role but also provides a good example for your young players who may model your behavior.

Physical contact can also be a very important use of body language. A handshake, a pat on the head, an arm around the shoulder, or even a big hug are effective ways of showing approval, concern, affection, and joy to your players. Youngsters are especially in need of this type of nonverbal message. Keep within the obvious moral and legal limits, but don't be reluctant to touch your players and send a message that can only truly be expressed in that way.

How Can I Improve My Receiving Skills?

Now, let's examine the other half of the communication process— receiving messages. Too often people are very good senders but very poor receivers of messages. As a coach of young athletes, it is essential that you are able to fulfill both roles effectively.

The requirements for receiving messages are quite simple, but receiving skills are perhaps less satisfying and therefore underdeveloped compared to sending skills. People seem to naturally enjoy hearing themselves talk more than others. But if you are willing to read about the keys to receiving messages and to make a strong effort to use them with your players, you'll be surprised by what you've been missing.

Attention!

First, you must pay attention; you must want to hear what others have to communicate to you. That's not always easy when you're busy coaching and have many things competing for your attention. But in one-to-one or team meetings with players, you must really focus on what they are telling you, both verbally and nonverbally. You'll be amazed at the little signals you pick up. Not only will such focused attention help you catch every word your players say, but you'll also notice your players' moods and physical states, and you'll get an idea of your players' feelings toward you and other players on the team.

Listen CARE-FULLY

How we receive messages from others, perhaps more than anything else we do, demonstrates how much we care for the sender and what that person has to tell us. If you care little for your players or have little regard for what they have to say, it will show in how you attend and listen to them. Check yourself. Do you find your mind wandering to what you are going to do after practice while one of your players is talking to you? Do you frequently have to ask your players, "What did you say?" If so, you need to work on your receiving mechanics of attending and listening.

But perhaps the most critical question you should ask yourself, if you find that you're missing the messages your players send, is this: Do I care?

How Do I Put It All Together?

So far we've discussed separately the sending and receiving of messages. But we all know that senders and receivers switch roles several times during an interaction. One person initiates a communication by sending a message to another person, who then receives the message. The receiver then switches roles and becomes the sender by responding to the person who sent the initial message. These verbal and nonverbal responses are called feedback.

Your players will be looking to you for feedback all the time. They will want to know how you think they are performing, what you think of their ideas, and whether their efforts please you. Obviously, you can respond in many different ways. How you respond will strongly affect your players. So let's take a look at a few general types of feedback and examine their possible effects.

Providing Instructions

With young players, much of your feedback will involve answering questions about how to play basketball. Your instructive responses to these questions should include both verbal and nonverbal feedback. Here are some suggestions for giving instructional feedback:

- Keep verbal instructions simple and concise.

- Use demonstrations to provide nonverbal instructional feedback (see unit 4).

- "Walk" players through the skill, or use a slow-motion demonstration if they are having trouble learning.

Correcting Errors

When your players perform incorrectly, you need to provide informative feedback to correct the error—and the sooner the better. When you do correct errors, keep in mind these two principles: Use negative criticism sparingly, and keep calm.

Use Negative Criticism Sparingly

Although you may need to punish players for horseplay or dangerous activities by scolding or removing them from activity temporarily, avoid reprimanding players for performance errors. Admonishing players for honest mistakes makes them afraid to even try. Nothing ruins a youngster's enjoyment of a sport more than a coach who harps on every miscue. So instead, correct your players by using the positive approach. Your players will enjoy playing more, and you'll enjoy coaching more.

Keep Calm

Don't fly off the handle when your players make mistakes. Remember, you're coaching young and inexperienced players, not pros. You'll therefore see more incorrect than correct technique, and you'll probably have more discipline problems than you expect. But throwing a tantrum over each error or misbehavior will only inhibit your players or suggest to them the wrong kind of behavior to model. So let your players know that mistakes aren't the end of the world; stay cool!

Positive Feedback

Praising players when they have performed or behaved well is an effective way of getting them to repeat (or try to repeat) that behavior in the future. Positive feedback for effort is an especially effective way to motivate youngsters to work on difficult skills. So rather than shouting and providing negative feedback to a player who has made a mistake, try offering players a compliment sandwich, described on page 22.

Sometimes just the way you word feedback can make it more positive than negative. For example, instead of saying, "Don't shoot the ball that way," you might say, "Shoot the ball this way." Then your players will be focusing on what to do instead of what not to do.

You can give positive feedback verbally and nonverbally. Telling a player, especially in front of teammates, that he or she has performed well is a great way to boost the confidence of a youngster. And a pat on the back or a handshake can be a very tangible way of communicating your recognition of a player's performance.

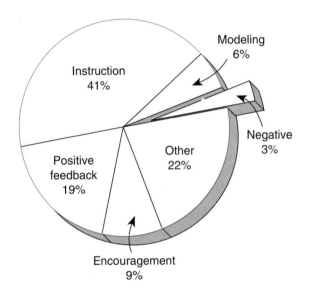

Coaches, be positive!

Only a very small percentage of ASEP-trained coaches' behaviors are negative.

Who Else Do I Need to Communicate With?

Coaching involves not only sending and receiving messages and providing proper feedback to players, but also interacting with parents, fans, game officials, and opposing coaches. If you don't communicate effectively with these groups of people, your coaching career will be unpleasant and short-lived. So try the following suggestions for communicating with these groups.

Parents

A player's parents need to be assured that their son or daughter is under the direction of a coach who is both knowledgeable about the sport and concerned about the youngster's well-being. You can put their worries to rest by holding a preseason parent orientation meeting in which you describe your background and your approach to coaching.

If parents contact you with a concern during the season, listen to them closely and try to offer positive responses. If you need to communicate with parents, catch them after a practice, give them a phone call, or send a note through the mail. Messages sent to parents through children are too often lost, misinterpreted, or forgotten.

Fans

The stands probably won't be overflowing at your games, but that only means that you'll more easily hear the few fans who criticize your coaching. When you hear something negative said about the job you're doing, don't respond. Keep calm, consider whether the message had any value, and if not, forget it. Acknowledging critical, unwarranted comments from a fan during a contest will only encourage others to voice their opinions. So put away your "rabbit ears" and communicate to fans, through your actions, that you are a confident, competent coach.

Prepare your players for fans' criticisms. Tell them it is you, not the spectators, to whom they should listen. If you notice that one of your players is rattled by a fan's comment, reassure the player that your evaluation is more objective and favorable—and the one that counts.

Game Officials

How you communicate with officials will have a great influence on the way your players behave toward them. Therefore you need to set an example. Greet officials with a handshake, an introduction, and perhaps some casual conversation about the upcoming contest. Indicate your respect for them before, during, and after the contest. Don't make nasty remarks, shout, or use disrespectful body gestures. Your players will see you do it, and they'll get the idea that such behavior is appropriate. Plus, if the official hears or sees you, the communication between the two of you will break down.

Opposing Coaches

Make an effort to visit with the coach of the opposing team before the game. Perhaps the two of you can work out a special arrangement for the contest, such as free substitution of players. During the game, don't get into a personal feud with the opposing coach. Remember, it's the kids, not the coaches, who are competing. And by getting along well with the opposing coach, you'll show your players that competition involves cooperation.

✔ Summary Checklist

Now, check your coach-communication skills by answering "Yes" or "No" to the following questions.

	Yes	No
1. Are your verbal messages to your players positive and honest?	___	___
2. Do you speak loudly, clearly, and in a language your athletes understand?	___	___
3. Do you remember to repeat instructions to your players, in case they didn't hear you the first time?	___	___

	Yes	No

4. Are the tone of your voice and your nonverbal messages consistent with the words you use? ____ ____

5. Do your facial expressions and body language express interest in and happiness with your coaching role? ____ ____

6. Are you attentive to your players and able to pick up even their small verbal and nonverbal cues? ____ ____

7. Do you really care about what your athletes say to you? ____ ____

8. Do you instruct rather than criticize when your players make errors? ____ ____

9. Are you usually positive when responding to things your athletes say and do? ____ ____

10. Do you try to communicate in a cooperative and respectful manner with players' parents, fans, game officials, and opposing coaches? ____ ____

If you answered "No" to any of the above questions, you may want to refer back to the section of the chapter where the topic was discussed. Now is the time to address communication problems, not when you're coaching young athletes.

How Do I Get My Team Ready to Play?

To coach basketball, you must understand the basic rules, skills, and strategies of the sport. The second part of this book provides the basic information you'll need to comprehend the sport.

But all the basketball knowledge in the world will do you little good unless you present it effectively to your players. That's why this unit is so important. Here you will learn the steps to take when teaching sport skills, as well as practical guidelines for planning your season and individual practices.

How Do I Teach Sport Skills?

Many people believe that the only qualification needed to coach is to have played the sport. It's helpful to have played, but there is much more to coaching successfully. Even if you haven't played or even watched basketball, you can still learn to coach successfully with this IDEA:

I—Introduce the skill.

D—Demonstrate the skill.

E—Explain the skill.

A—Attend to players practicing the skill.

Introduce the Skill

Players, especially young and inexperienced ones, need to know what skill they are learning and why they are learning it. You should therefore take these three steps every time you introduce a skill to your players:

1. Get your players' attention.

2. Name the skill.

3. Explain the importance of the skill.

Get Your Players' Attention

Because youngsters are easily distracted, use some method to get their attention. Some coaches use interesting news items or stories. Others use jokes. And others simply project enthusiasm that gets their players to listen. Whatever method you use, speak slightly above the normal volume and look your players in the eyes when you speak.

Also, position players so they can see and hear you. Arrange the players in two or three evenly spaced rows, facing you and not some source of distraction. Then ask if everyone can see you before you begin.

Name the Skill

Although you might mention other common names for the skill, decide which one you'll use and stick with it. This will help avoid confusion and enhance communication among your players.

Explain the Importance of the Skill

Although the importance of a skill may be apparent to you, your players may be less able to see how the skill will help them become better basketball players. Offer them a reason for learning the skill and describe how the skill relates to more advanced skills.

> *"The most difficult aspect of coaching is this: Coaches must learn to let athletes learn. Sport skills should be taught so they have meaning to the child, not just meaning to the coach."*
>
> Rainer Martens, ASEP Founder

Demonstrate the Skill

The demonstration step is the most important part of teaching sport skills to young players who may have never done anything closely resembling the skill. They need a picture, not just words. They need to see how the skill is performed.

If you are unable to perform the skill correctly, have an assistant coach, one of your players, or someone skilled in basketball perform the demonstration. These tips will help make your demonstrations more effective:

- Use correct form.
- Demonstrate the skill several times.
- Slow down the action, if possible, during one or two performances so players can see every movement involved in the skill.
- Perform the skill at different angles so your players can get a full perspective of it.
- Demonstrate the skill with both the right and left hands.

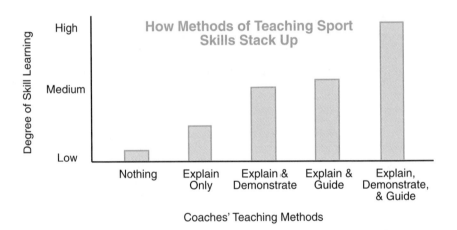

Explain the Skill

Players learn more effectively when they're given a brief explanation of the skill along with the demonstration. Use simple terms and, if possible, relate the skill to previously learned skills. Ask your players whether they understand your description. A good technique is to ask the team to repeat your explanation. Ask questions like "What are you going to do first?" "Then what?" Watch for looks of confusion or uncertainty and repeat your explanation and demonstration of those points. If possible, use different words so that your players get a chance to try to understand from a different perspective.

Complex skills often are better understood when they are explained in more manageable parts. For instance, if you want to teach your players how to change direction when they dribble the ball, you might take the following steps:

1. Show them a correct performance of the entire skill, and explain its function in basketball.
2. Break down the skill and point out its component parts to your players.
3. Have players perform each of the component skills you have already taught them, such as dribbling while running, switching dribbling hands while keeping their heads up, and planting and pushing off a foot to change direction.
4. After players have demonstrated their ability to perform the separate parts of the skill in sequence, reexplain the entire skill.
5. Have players practice the skill.

One caution: Young players have short attention spans, and a long demonstration or explanation of the skill will bore them. So spend no more than a few minutes combined on the introduction, demonstration, and explanation phases. Then get the players active in attempts to perform the skill. The total IDEA should be completed in 10 minutes or less, followed by individual and group practice activities.

Attend to Players Practicing the Skill

If the skill you selected was within your players' capabilities, and you have done an effective job of introducing, demonstrating, and explaining it, your players should be ready to attempt the skill. Some players may need to be physically guided through the movements during their first few attempts. Walking unsure athletes through the skill in this way will help them gain confidence to perform the skill on their own.

Your teaching duties don't end when all your athletes have demonstrated that they understand how to perform the skill. In fact, a significant part of your teaching will involve observing closely the hit-and-miss trial performances of your players.

As you observe players' efforts in drills and activities, offer positive, corrective feedback in the form of the "compliment sandwich" described in unit 3. If a player performs the skill properly, acknowledge it and offer praise. Keep in mind that your feedback will have a great influence on your players' motivation to practice and improve their performance.

Remember, too, that young players need individual instruction. So set aside a time before, during, or after practice to give individual help.

What Planning Do I Need to Do?

Beginning coaches often make the mistake of showing up for the first practice with no particular plan in mind. These coaches find that their practices are unorganized, their players are frustrated and inattentive, and the amount and quality of their skill instruction is limited. Planning is essential to successful teaching and coaching. And it doesn't begin on the way to practice!

Preseason Planning

Effective coaches begin planning well before the start of the season. Among the preseason measures that will make the season more enjoyable, successful, and safe for you and your players are the following:

- Familiarize yourself with the sport organization you are involved in, especially its philosophy and goals regarding youth sport.

- Examine the availability of facilities, equipment, instructional aids, and other materials needed for practices and games.

- Find out what fund-raising you and your players will be expected to do, and decide on the best way to meet your goals.

- Make arrangements for any team travel that will be required during the season. Consider clearance forms, supervision, transportation, equipment, contacting parents, and safety.

- Check to see whether you have adequate liability insurance to cover you when one of your players gets hurt (see unit 5). If you don't, get some.

- Establish your coaching priorities regarding having fun, developing players' skills, and winning.

- Select and meet with your assistant coaches to discuss the philosophy, goals, team rules, and plans for the season.

- Register players for the team. Have them complete a player information form and obtain medical clearance forms, if required.

- Institute an injury-prevention program for your players.

- Hold an orientation meeting to inform parents of your background, philosophy, goals, and instructional approach. Also, give a brief overview of basketball rules, terms, and strategies to familiarize parents or guardians with the sport.

You may be surprised at the number of things you should do even before the first practice. But if you address them during the preseason, the season will be much more enjoyable and productive for you and your players.

In-Season Planning

Your choice of activities during the season should be based on whether they will help your players develop physical and mental skills, knowledge of rules and game tactics, sportsmanship, and love for the sport. All of these goals are important, but we'll focus on the skills and tactics of basketball to give you an idea of how to itemize your objectives.

Goal Setting

What you plan to do during the season must be reasonable for the maturity and skill level of your players. In terms of basketball skills and tactics, you should teach young players the basics and move on to more complex activities only after the players have mastered these easier techniques and strategies.

To begin the season, your instructional goals might include the following:

- Players will be able to assume and maintain the ready position.
- Players will be able to dribble with either hand.
- Players will be able to shoot a layup correctly from both sides of the basket.
- Players will be able to make accurate chest and bounce passes to stationary and moving teammates.
- Players will be able to catch passes while stationary or moving.
- Players will be able to maintain control of the dribble while running.
- Players will be able to set effective screens on the ball and away from the ball.
- Players will be able to position themselves and then slide their feet to guard an opposing dribbler.
- Players will be able to position themselves correctly to guard opponents away from the ball.
- Players will be able to perform a set or jump shot using correct shooting technique.
- Players will demonstrate knowledge of basketball rules.
- Players will demonstrate knowledge of basic offensive and defensive strategies.

Organizing

After you've defined the skills and tactics you want your players to learn during the season, you can plan how to teach them to your players in practices. But be flexible! If your players are having difficulty learning a skill or tactic, take some extra time until they get the hang of it—even if that means moving back your schedule. After all, if your players are unable to perform the fundamental skills, they'll never execute the more complex skills you have scheduled for them, and they won't have much fun trying.

Still, it helps to have a plan for progressing players through skills during the season. The 4-week sample season plan in Appendix A shows how to schedule your skill instruction in an organized and progressive manner. If this is your first coaching experience, you may wish to follow the plan as it stands. If you have some previous experience, you may want to modify the schedule to better fit the needs of your team.

The way you organize your season may also help your players to develop socially and psychologically. By giving your players responsibility for certain aspects of practices—leading warm-up and stretching activities are common examples—you help players to develop self-esteem and take responsibility for themselves and the team. As you plan your season, consider ways to provide your players with experiences that lead them to steadily improve these skills.

What Makes Up a Good Practice?

A good instructional plan makes practice preparation much easier. Have players work on more important and less difficult goals in early-season practice sessions. See to it that players master basic skills before moving on to more advanced ones.

It is helpful to establish one goal for each practice, but try to include a variety of activities related to that goal. For example, although your primary objective might be to improve players' dribbling skills, you should have players perform several different drills designed to enhance that single skill. To add more variety to your practices, vary the order of the activities.

In general, we recommend that in each of your practices you do the following:

- *Warm up.*
- *Practice previously taught skills.*
- *Teach and practice new skills.*
- *Practice under competitive conditions.*
- *Cool down.*
- *Evaluate.*

Warm Up

As you're checking the roster and announcing the performance goals for the practice, your players should be preparing their bodies for vigorous activity. A 5- to 10-minute period of easy-paced activities, stretching, and calisthenics should be sufficient for youngsters to limber their muscles and reduce the risk of injury.

Practice Previously Taught Skills

Devote part of each practice to having players work on the fundamental skills they already know. But remember, kids like variety. Thus you should organize and modify drills so that everyone is involved and stays interested. Praise and encourage players when you notice improvement, and offer individual assistance to those who need help.

Teach and Practice New Skills

Gradually build on your players' existing skills by giving players something new to practice each session. The proper method for teaching sport skills is described on pages 36–40. Refer to those pages if you have any questions about teaching new skills or if you want to evaluate your teaching approach periodically during the season.

Practice Under Competitive Conditions

Competition among teammates during practices prepares players for actual games and informs young athletes about their abilities relative to their peers. Youngsters also seem to have more fun in competitive activities.

You can create game-like conditions by using competitive drills, modified games, and scrimmages (see units 7 and 8). However, consider the following guidelines before introducing competition into your practices:

- All players should have an equal opportunity to participate.
- Match players by ability and physical maturity.
- Make sure that players can execute fundamental skills before they compete in groups.
- Emphasize performing well, not winning, in every competition.
- Give players room to make mistakes by avoiding constant evaluation of their performances.

Cool Down

Each practice should wind down with a 5- to 10-minute period of light exercise, including jogging, performance of simple skills, and some stretching. The cool-down allows athletes' bodies to return to the resting state and avoid stiffness, and it affords you an opportunity to review the practice.

Evaluate

At the end of practice spend a few minutes with your players reviewing how well the session accomplished the goals you had set. Even if your evaluation is negative, show optimism for future practices and send players off on an upbeat note.

How Do I Put a Practice Together?

Simply knowing the six practice components is not enough. You must also be able to arrange those components into a logical progression and fit them into a time schedule. Now, using your instructional goals as a guide for selecting what skills to have your players work on, try to plan several basketball practices you might conduct. The following example should help you get started.

Sample Practice Plan

Performance Objective. Players will be able to throw effective chest and bounce passes.

Component	Time	Activity or drill
Warm up	10 min	Full-court dribbling Calisthenics
Practice	20 min	Pass and Move Drill Shotgun Drill
Teach	15 min	Two-hand chest and bounce passing with a partner, stationary, and running full-court
Scrimmage	15 min	3-on-3 scrimmage
Cool down and evaluate	10 min	Easy jogging Free throws Stretching

✔ *Summary Checklist*

During your basketball season, check your planning and teaching skills periodically. As you gain more coaching experience, you should be able to answer "Yes" to each of the following.

When you plan, do you remember to plan for

____ preseason events such as player registration, fund-raising, travel, liability protection, use of facilities, and parent orientation?

____ season goals such as the development of players' physical skills, mental skills, sportsmanship, and enjoyment?

____ practice components such as warm-up, practicing previously taught skills, teaching and practicing new skills, practicing under game-like conditions, cool-down, and evaluation?

When you teach sport skills to your players, do you

____ arrange the players so everyone can see and hear?

____ introduce the skill clearly and explain its importance?

____ demonstrate the skill properly several times?

____ explain the skill simply and accurately?

____ attend closely to players practicing the skill?

____ offer corrective, positive feedback or praise after observing players' attempts at the skill?

What About Safety?

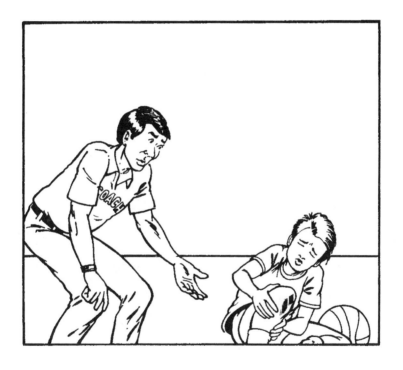

One of your players appears to break free downcourt, dribbling the ball toward the basket for an apparent layup. Out of nowhere races a defender who catches up with and accidentally undercuts your player. You see that your player is not getting up and seems to be in pain. What do you do?

No coach wants to see players get hurt. But injury remains a reality of sport participation; consequently, you must be prepared to provide first aid when injuries occur and to protect yourself against unjustified lawsuits. Fortunately, there are many preventive measures coaches can institute to reduce the risk. This unit will describe how you can

- create the safest possible environment for your players,
- provide emergency first aid to players when they get hurt, and
- protect yourself from injury liability.

How Do I Keep My Players From Getting Hurt?

Injuries may occur because of poor preventive measures. Part of your planning, described in unit 4, should include steps that give your players the best possible chance for injury-free participation. These steps include the following:

- *Preseason physical examination*
- *Nutrition*
- *Physical conditioning*
- *Equipment and facilities inspection*
- *Matching athletes by physical maturity and warning of inherent risks*
- *Proper supervision and record keeping*
- *Providing water breaks*
- *Warm-up and cool-down*

Preseason Physical Examination

In the absence of severe injury or ongoing illness, your players should have a physical examination every 2 years. If a player has a known complication, a physician's consent should be obtained before participation is allowed. You should also have players' parents or guardians sign a participation agreement form and a release form to allow their children to be treated in the case of an emergency.

INFORMED CONSENT FORM

I hereby give my permission for _____ to participate

in _____ during the athletic season beginning in 199____.
Further, I authorize the school to provide emergency treatment of an injury to or illness of my child if qualified medical personnel consider treatment necessary *and* perform the treatment. This authorization is granted only if I cannot be reached and a reasonable effort has been made to do so.

Date _____   Parent or guardian _____

Address _____ Phone ( ) _____

Family physician _____ Phone ( ) _____

Pre-existing medical conditions (e.g., allergies or chronic illnesses) _____

_____

Other(s) to also contact in case of emergency _____

Relationship to child _____ Phone ( ) _____

My child and I are aware that participating in _____
is a potentially hazardous activity. I assume all risks associated with participation in this sport, including but not limited to falls, contact with other participants, the effects of the weather, traffic, and other reasonable risk conditions associated with the sport. All such risks to my child are known and understood by me.

I understand this informed consent form and agree to its conditions on behalf of my child.

Child's signature _____ Date _____

Parent's signature _____ Date _____

Nutrition

Increasingly, disordered eating and unhealthy dietary habits are affecting youth basketball players. Let players and parents know the importance of healthy eating and the dangers that can arise from efforts to lose weight too quickly. Young basketball players need to supply their bodies with the extra energy they require to keep up with the demands of practices and games. Ask your director about information that you can pass on to your players and their parents, and include a discussion of basic, commonsense nutrition in your parent orientation meeting.

Physical Conditioning

Muscles, tendons, and ligaments unaccustomed to vigorous and long-lasting physical activity are prone to injury. Therefore, prepare your athletes to withstand the exertion of playing your sport. An effective conditioning program for basketball would involve running and other forms of aerobic activity.

Make conditioning drills and activities fun. Include a skill component, such as dribbling, to prevent players from becoming bored or looking upon the activity as work.

Keep in mind, too, that players on your team may respond differently to conditioning activities. Wide-ranging levels of fitness or natural ability might mean that an activity that challenges one child is beyond another's ability to complete safely. The environment is another factor that may affect players' responses to activity. The same workout that was effective on a cool morning might be hazardous to players on a hot, humid afternoon. Similarly, an activity children excel in at sea level might present a risk at higher altitudes. An ideal conditioning program prepares players for the season's demands without neglecting physical and environmental factors that affect their safety.

Equipment and Facilities Inspection

Another way to prevent injuries is to check the quality and fit of all of the protective equipment used by your players. Slick-soled, poor fitting, or unlaced basketball shoes; unstrapped eyeglasses; and jewelry are dangerous on the basketball court—both to the player wearing such items and to other participants. Encourage players to switch into their basketball shoes when they reach practice and game sites so that the soles of their shoes are free of mud and moisture.

Remember, also, to examine regularly the court on which your players practice and play. Wipe up wet spots, remove hazards, report conditions you cannot remedy, and request maintenance as necessary. If unsafe conditions exist, either make adaptations to avoid risk to your players' safety or stop the practice or game until safe conditions have been restored.

Matching Athletes by Maturity and Warning of Inherent Risks

Children of the same age may differ in height and weight by up to 6 inches and 50 pounds. That's why in contact sports, or sports in which size provides an advantage, it's essential to match players against opponents of similar size and physical maturity. Such an approach gives smaller, less mature children a better chance to succeed and avoid injury, and provides larger children with more of a challenge.

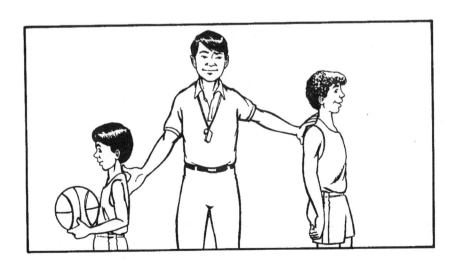

Matching helps protect you from certain liability concerns. But you also must warn players of the inherent risks involved in playing basketball, because "failure to warn" is one of the most successful arguments in lawsuits against coaches. So, thoroughly explain the inherent risks of basketball, and make sure each player knows, understands, and appreciates those risks.

ASEP Fact

Basketball is one of the top four injury-producing sports participated in by young athletes.

The preseason parent orientation meeting is a good opportunity to explain the risks of the sport to parents and players. It is also a good occasion on which to have both the players and their parents sign waivers releasing you from liability should an injury occur. Such waivers do not relieve you of responsibility for your players' well-being, but they are recommended by lawyers.

Proper Supervision and Record Keeping

With youngsters, your mere presence in the area of play is not enough; you must actively plan and direct team activities and closely observe and evaluate players' participation. You're the watchdog responsible for the players' well-being. So if you notice a player limping or grimacing, give him or her a rest and examine the extent of the injury.

As a coach, you're also required to enforce the rules of the sport, prohibit dangerous horseplay, and hold practices only under safe weather conditions. These specific supervisory activities will make the play environment safer for your players and will help protect you from liability if a mishap does occur.

For further protection, keep records of your season plans, practice plans, and players' injuries. Season and practice plans come in handy when you need evidence that players have been taught certain skills, whereas accurate, detailed accident report forms offer protection against unfounded lawsuits. Ask for these forms from the organization to which you belong. And hold onto these records for several years so that an "old basketball injury" of a former player doesn't come back to haunt you.

Providing Water Breaks

Encourage players to drink plenty of water before, during, and after practice. Because water makes up 45% to 65% of a youngster's body weight, and water weighs about a pound per pint, the loss of even a little water can have severe consequences for the body's systems. And it doesn't have to be hot and humid for players to become dehydrated. Nor do players have to feel thirsty; in fact, by the time they are aware of their thirst, they are long overdue for a drink.

Warm-Up and Cool-Down

Although young bodies are generally very limber, they, too, can get tight from inactivity. Therefore, a warm-up period of approximately 10 minutes before each practice is strongly recommended. Warm-up should address each muscle group and get the heart rate elevated in preparation for strenuous activity. Easy running followed by stretching activities is a common sequence.

As practice is winding down, slow players' heart rates with an easy jog or walk. Then arrange for a 5- to 10-minute period of easy stretching at the end of practice to help players avoid stiff muscles and make them less tight before the next practice.

What if One of My Players Gets Hurt?

No matter how good and thorough your prevention program, injuries will occur. When injury does strike, chances are you will be the one in charge. The severity and nature of the injury will determine how actively involved you'll be in treating the injury. But regardless of how seriously a player is hurt, it is your responsibility to know what steps to take. So let's look at how you can provide basic emergency care to your injured athletes.

ASEP Fact

Approximately 40% of all injuries in boys' basketball involve players' ankles and feet.

Minor Injuries

Although no injury seems minor to the person experiencing it, most injuries are neither life threatening nor severe enough to restrict participation. When such injuries occur, you can take an active role in their initial treatment.

ASEP Fact

You shouldn't let a fear of acquired immune deficiency syndrome (AIDS) stop you from helping a player. On the court you are only at risk if you allow contaminated blood to come in contact with an open wound, so the blood barrier that you wear will protect you from AIDS should one of your players carry this disease. Check with your director or ASEP for more information about protecting yourself and your participants from AIDS.

Scrapes and Cuts

When one of your players has an open wound, the first thing you should do is to put on a pair of disposable surgical gloves or some other effective blood barrier. Then follow these four steps:

1. Stop the bleeding by applying direct pressure with a clean dressing to the wound and elevating it. The player may be able to apply this pressure while you put on your gloves. Do not remove the dressing if it becomes soaked with blood. Instead, place an additional dressing on top of the one already in place. If bleeding continues, elevate the injured area above the heart and maintain pressure.

2. Cleanse the wound thoroughly once the bleeding is controlled. A good rinsing with a forceful stream of water, and perhaps light scrubbing with soap, will help prevent infection.

3. Protect the wound with sterile gauze or a bandage. If the player continues to participate, apply protective padding over the injured area.

4. Remove and dispose of gloves carefully to prevent you or anyone else from coming into contact with blood.

For bloody noses not associated with serious facial injury, have the athlete sit and lean slightly forward. Then pinch the player's nostrils shut. If the bleeding continues after several minutes, or if the athlete has a history of nosebleeds, seek medical assistance.

Strains and Sprains

The physical demands of basketball practices and games often result in injury to the muscles or tendons (strains), or to the ligaments (sprains). When your players suffer minor strains or sprains, immediately apply the PRICE method of injury care (see page 58).

Bumps and Bruises

Inevitably, basketball players make contact with each other and with the court. If the force of a body part at impact is great enough, a bump or bruise will result. Many players continue playing with such sore spots, but if the bump or bruise is large and painful, you should

The PRICE Method

P—Protect the athlete and injured body part from further danger or further trauma.

R—Rest the area to avoid further damage and foster healing.

I —Ice the area to reduce swelling and pain.

C—Compress the area by securing an ice bag in place with an elastic wrap.

E—Elevate the injury above heart level to keep the blood from pooling in the area.

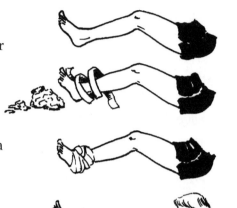

act appropriately. Enact the PRICE method for injury care and monitor the injury. If swelling, discoloration, and pain have lessened, the player may resume participation with protective padding; if not, the player should be examined by a physician.

Serious Injuries

Head, neck, and back injuries; fractures; and injuries that cause a player to lose consciousness are among a class of injuries that you cannot, and should not, try to treat yourself. But you should plan for what you'll do if such an injury occurs. Your plan should include the following guidelines for action:

- Obtain the phone number and ensure the availability of nearby emergency care units. Include this information as part of a written emergency plan before the season, and have it with you at every practice and game.

- Assign an assistant coach or another adult the responsibility of knowing the location of the nearest phone and contacting emergency medical help upon your request.
- Ensure that emergency medical information, treatment, and transportation consent forms are available during every practice and match.
- Do not move the injured athlete.
- Calm the injured athlete and keep others away from him or her as much as possible.
- Evaluate whether the athlete's breathing is stopped or irregular, and if necessary, clear the airway with your fingers.
- Administer artificial respiration if breathing is stopped. Administer cardiopulmonary resuscitation (CPR), or have a trained individual administer CPR if the athlete's circulation has stopped.
- Remain with the athlete until medical personnel arrive.

ASEP Fact

Nearly 90% of girls' basketball injuries that require surgery involve the knee.

How Do I Protect Myself?

When one of your players is injured, naturally your first concern is his or her well-being. Your feelings for children, after all, are what made you decide to coach. Unfortunately, there is something else that you must consider: Can you be held liable for the injury?

From a legal standpoint, a coach has nine duties to fulfill. We've discussed all but planning (see unit 4) in this unit:

1. Provide a safe environment.
2. Properly plan the activity.
3. Provide adequate and proper equipment.
4. Match or equate athletes.
5. Warn of inherent risks in the sport.
6. Supervise the activity closely.

7. Evaluate athletes for injury or incapacitation.

8. Know emergency procedures and first aid.

9. Keep adequate records.

In addition to fulfilling these nine legal duties, you should check your insurance coverage to make sure your policy will protect you from liability.

Summary Self-Test

Now that you've read how to make your coaching experience safe for your players and yourself, test your knowledge of the material by answering these questions:

1. What are eight injury-prevention measures you can institute to try to keep your players from getting hurt?
2. What is the four-step emergency care process for cuts?
3. What method of treatment is best for minor sprains and strains?
4. What steps can you take to manage serious injuries?
5. What are the nine legal duties of a coach?

What Is Basketball All About?

From reading the first part of this book, you now have a good, general understanding of what it takes to coach. Now it's time to develop your comprehension of basketball. This part of the book provides the basketball-specific information you will need to teach your players the sport.

Basketball Coaching: Worth a Shot

You probably played or watched basketball before you agreed to coach it. But whether you were a high school star or an infrequent observer, you'll need a new perspective on the sport to teach it effectively to young players. If you were a player, you had to be concerned about only one role on the team—your own. Now you must consider not only your own coaching role, but every player's role on the team. Furthermore, you must help all of your players to learn and fulfill their roles.

So why take the time and trouble to coach basketball? Perhaps the best reason is because kids love the sport. Give youngsters a basketball and a hoop, and they'll play until they drop. Kids' fondness for the sport is both a plus and a minus, though, in your effort to coach them. On the plus side, their interest and previous experience playing the sport should make them eager and somewhat prepared students of the game. On the minus side, having watched older, bigger, and much more skilled players perform, the youngsters may think they know more about the skills and strategies of the sport than they actually do. Therefore, they may be less motivated to learn the basics of the sport.

ASEP Fact

U.S. kids rank basketball as their #1 team sport.

Your challenge as a youth basketball coach is to teach your players the fundamentals of the sport and to maintain their attention and interest, while still allowing them to have fun. To meet this challenge, read the rest of this manual and then take your players to the HOOP:

> H—Hold their attention with brief instruction and lots of activity.
>
> O—Organize practices so players can both learn and have fun.
>
> O—Opt for fulfilling players' needs rather than winning at all costs.
>
> P—Provide a good model in skill demonstrations and courtside behavior.

What Are the Rules?

Basketball rules vary slightly at each level of play. Modifications are made to suit the size, skill, and age of the participants. Your team will play by rules similar to those established by the National Federation of State High School Associations, but check with the directors of your league before the season to learn of any unique guidelines they may have instituted. If you do your homework and communicate the rules well to your team, your players won't be caught unaware in games. In the eyes of your players, your credibility will also increase if they are confident of your knowledge of the rules.

Ball and Court Dimensions

Because basketball is a game in which a ball is passed, dribbled, and shot with the hands, the size of the ball must be appropriate for participants. A regulation men's basketball is far too heavy and large for kids to handle. Your league will probably use a standard women's basketball (18 to 20 ounces and 28.5 to 29.0 inches in circumference), or an even smaller ball that is made specifically for youth leagues.

Scaled-down courts let kids compete without getting too tired. We also recommend lowering the basket height, so that even the youngest players can get the ball to the hoop by shooting, not throwing, the ball and experience success (see Figure 6.1).

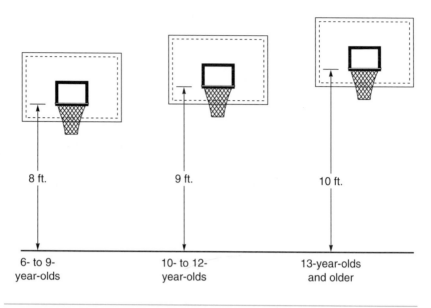

8 ft.

9 ft.

10 ft.

6- to 9-
year-olds

10- to 12-
year-olds

13-year-olds
and older

■ **Figure 6.1** Recommended basket heights for youth basketball.

Court Markings

Regardless of the size of the court, specific areas of the floor are designated for certain game activities or restrictions. For instance, the free throw lane indicates where offensive players can spend no more than 3 seconds consecutively while their team is in control of the ball. Take time to familiarize yourself with the court markings illustrated in Figure 6.2.

Several areas of the court are referred to with special basketball terminology. The term *frontcourt* refers to the half of the court where your team's offensive basket is located. The *backcourt* includes the midcourt line and the half of the court where your opponent's basket is located. The *3-second lane* area extends from the baseline under the basket to the free throw line. This is also called the *key*. The semicircle that extends beyond the free throw line designates the *top of the key*. Any activity outside the 3-second lane area is said to occur on the *perimeter*. The *3-point line* marks a semicircle that is 19 feet from the basket at all points. Finally, the square markings 6 feet from the baseline on each side of the lane are referred to as the *blocks*.

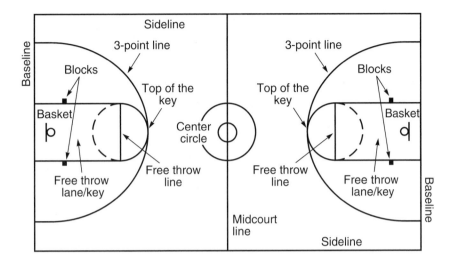

■ **Figure 6.2** Basketball court.

Player Equipment

Basketball requires very little equipment. Basketball shoes are necessary for proper traction on the court, and two pairs of athletic socks are recommended to avoid blisters. Athletic shorts and tank tops or loose fitting shirts allow players the freedom of movement needed to run, jump, and shoot. Soft pads may be advised for players with conditions involving the knees or elbows. Safety glasses or goggles may be worn to protect the eyes from injury.

Player Positions

Basketball is played with five players per team (although some youth leagues play 3-on-3 or 4-on-4). During the course of a game, each player alternates between offense (when the player's own team has the ball and is trying to score a basket) and defense (when the opposing team has the ball, and the player's team is trying to prevent the other team from scoring a basket). The three general positions in basketball are commonly classified as guard, forward, and center (see Figure 6.3).

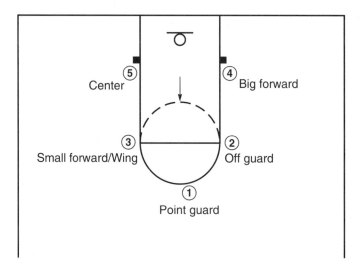

Figure 6.3 Player positions.

Guards

Guards usually are the best ballhandlers and outside shooters on the team. They tend to be shorter and quicker than the other players and have good dribbling and passing skills. Guards play farthest from the basket, on the perimeter.

A basketball team usually has two guards in the game at all times. The point guard, or #1 position, is filled by the team's best dribbler and passer. The other guard position, the off guard or #2 position, is often the team's best long-range shooter and second-best dribbler.

Forwards

Forwards typically are taller than guards and play near the basket. Forwards should be able to shoot the ball accurately from within 12 feet of the basket and rebound the ball when shots are missed.

A team usually plays with two forwards in its lineup. The small forward (also referred to as the wing), or #3 position, is often filled by the most versatile and athletic member of the team. The small forward must be able to play in the lane and on the perimeter on offense, and to guard small and quick or big and strong opponents on defense. The other forward position, the big forward or #4 position, is a good spot to assign to one of your bigger players and better rebounders who can also shoot the ball from anywhere in the lane area.

Center

The center, or #5 position, also referred to as the post, is frequently the tallest or biggest player on the team. That extra size is helpful in maneuvering for shots or rebounds around the basket. A tall center can also make it difficult for opposing teams to shoot near the basket. A center should have "soft" hands to catch the passes thrown into the lane area by guards and forwards. Most basketball teams designate one player on the court as their center.

Alternate Positions

Below the high school level, players should be given an opportunity to play more than one position. Obviously, you're not likely to play your smallest guard at center. And if you constantly shuffle players from one spot to another, they'll get confused. However, that doesn't mean you should have players stay at one position throughout the whole season.

Table 6.1 shows a sample system for alternating players among positions.

Table 6.1
Sample System for Alternating Players Among Positions

Primary position	Alternate position(s)
#1—Point guard	Off guard
#2—Off guard	Small forward, point guard
#3—Small forward	Off guard, big forward
#4—Big forward	Center, small forward
#5—Center	Big forward

Officials

A youth basketball game is officiated by two individuals who should know the rules and enforce them to ensure a safe, fair, and fun contest. Officials should also require sportsmanship from all players and their coaches. You can be a big help to officials by respecting their efforts and emphasizing to your players the need to play with respect for the rules.

Appendix B shows the signals used by basketball officials during a game. Familiarize yourself with these signals and explain them to your players.

Length of the Game

Basketball games consist of two halves or four quarters. The game clock is stopped at halftime, between quarters, during time-outs, when the ball goes out of bounds, and when free throws are attempted. The length of the game should be adjusted according to the ages of the players. Youngsters 12 years old or under should play halves of no longer than 12 minutes. However, many youth leagues allow the clock to run continuously (except during time-outs and foul shots), so they play 16- to 20-minute halves.

Starting and Restarting the Game

A jump ball at center court is used to start games and overtime periods, which are played when teams are tied at the end of regulation time. During jump balls, each team has its center or best leaper attempt to tip the ball to a teammate (who must be outside of the center circle) to gain possession of the ball. In other jump ball situations, such as simultaneous possession of the ball by players from opposing teams, teams alternate possession; the team that did not win the first jump ball takes the ball out of bounds in the next jump ball situation.

Play stops not only during intermissions and time-outs, but also when the ball goes out of bounds and when an official calls a violation or foul. The clock restarts when the ball is touched following an inbounds pass or a missed free throw.

Fouls

Basketball can be a contact sport, with 10 players often in close proximity and in constant motion–running, cutting, and jumping. The rules of the game discourage rough play or tactics that allow a team to gain an advantage through brute force. Therefore, fouls are called when officials see illegal physical contact between two or more players based on these general principles:

- The first player to establish position (to become stationary or set) on the court has priority rights to that position.
- A body part cannot be extended into the path of an opponent.
- The player who moves into the path of an opponent–especially an airborne opponent–when contact occurs is responsible for the contact.
- All players have the right to the space extending straight up from their feet on the floor. This is called the principle of verticality.

Types of Fouls

Based on the general principles concerning player contact, these specific fouls are called in a game:

- *Blocking*—physically impeding the progress of another player who is still moving
- *Charging*—running into or pushing a defender who is stationary
- *Holding*—restricting movement of an opponent
- *Illegal screen*—a form of blocking in which the player setting the screen is still moving when the defender makes contact
- *Over-the-back*—infringing on the vertical plane of, and making contact with, a player who is in position and attempting to rebound
- *Reaching in*—extending an arm and making contact with a ballhandler in an attempt to steal the ball
- *Tripping*—extending a leg or foot and causing an opponent to lose balance or fall

The fouls listed are *personal* fouls. Certainly, this list is not all-inclusive, but it describes the most common kinds of fouls your players are likely to commit. The other fouls commonly committed in youth basketball are *shooting* fouls, where a defender makes contact with a player who is shooting the basketball. Emphasize to your players the importance of keeping hands off the shooter, establishing position, using feet more than arms to play defense, and not attempting to rebound over an opponent who has established position.

Officials may also call *intentional, technical,* or *flagrant* fouls. If you have been a good role model for your players and have communicated effectively to them the importance of proper conduct on and off the court, your players should not be cited for these types of fouls.

Consequences of Fouls

A team that fouls too much pays for it. Fouls carry with them increasingly severe penalties. A player with five fouls is disqualified from the game. And a team with more than a specified number of fouls in a quarter or half gives the opposing team a bonus situation: allowing it to shoot "one-and-one" free throws (FTs) for nonshooting fouls. (If the first FT is made, a second shot is awarded the shooter; if the first attempt is missed, play continues with the rebound off the shot.)

Table 6.2 lists the types of fouls and their consequences.

Table 6.2 Fouls and Consequences		
Type of foul	**Team fouled in bonus**	**Penalty**
Shooting	Yes/No	Two FTs
Personal	No	Ball out of bounds
Personal	Yes	One-and-one FTs
Intentional	Yes/No	Two FTs and ball out of bounds
Technical	Yes/No	Two FTs and ball out of bounds
Flagrant	Yes/No	Two FTs, fouler is disqualified, ball out of bounds

Communicating After Fouls

How you discuss fouls with players is important. Some coaches at the college and professional levels instruct their players to "get physical" with opponents. Such advice is inappropriate for youths. Discourage rough and dirty play. On the other hand, don't inhibit your players by making them fearful of fouling. Hustling young players will inevitably pick up some fouls in each game. When a foul is called, point out to the guilty player why the violation was called and explain to the player how the foul could have been avoided with a more effective action.

Violations

Ballhandling and time violations occur three to four times more often than fouls in youth basketball. The turnovers (loss of ball to the defense) caused by these violations will be one of your continuing frustrations as a basketball coach.

Ballhandling Violations

Here is a list of common miscues committed by young ballhandlers:

- *Double dribble*—resuming dribbling after having stopped dribbling (and no defender interrupts the player's possession of the ball) or dribbling with both hands at the same time
- *Charging*—described as a foul previously, but also recorded as a turnover by the offense
- *Over-and-back*—returning the ball to the backcourt by an offensive player after he or she has crossed into the frontcourt
- *Traveling*—taking more than one step without dribbling; also called "carrying the ball" or "palming the ball" as a player turns the ball a complete rotation in the hand between dribbles

Time Violations

Basketball games have many time restrictions that you'll need to inform your players of. Here's a list of time violations you'll want them to avoid:

- *10 seconds in backcourt*—The offensive team takes 10 or more seconds to get the ball across the midcourt line.
- *5 seconds inbound*—The offensive team fails to throw the ball within 5 seconds from the time the official hands the inbounder the ball. Time-outs must be called before the fourth count if a team is having trouble inbounding the ball.
- *5 seconds in possession*—An offensive player fails to get rid of the ball within 5 seconds after being guarded within 6 feet by a defender in the frontcourt.
- *3 seconds in the lane*—An offensive player is in the free throw lane of the frontcourt for 3 or more consecutive seconds while his or her team is in possession of the ball.

Other types of violations are possible, such as crossing the free throw line while shooting, or crossing the baseline or sideline while inbounding the ball. Make sure you inform your players of the proper guidelines, and encourage them to follow the same rules when practicing.

Communicating After Violations

John Wooden and other basketball coaches have distinguished between errors of commission and errors of omission. Errors of commission are mistakes associated with effort, such as a foul committed while hustling for a loose ball. Unless players are playing out of control, don't reprimand them after errors of commission. On the other hand, errors of omission–failures to perform assigned duties or within the rules–must be brought to the attention of the guilty player. It may be that the player simply was unaware of the role or rule that was not fulfilled. Whatever the case, calmly explain to the player what is necessary to correct the performance.

Scoring

Two points (assuming no 3-point line) are awarded for every field goal–that is, for every shot made that is not a free throw. A successful free throw is worth one point. The team that totals the most points over the course of the game is declared the winner.

Summary Test

Now that you've read the basic basketball information in this unit, you should be able to answer a number of questions about the sport. To test yourself, answer true (T) or false (F) to the following quiz questions:

1. _____ Over-the-back refers to a type of offensive turnover.

2. _____ The frontcourt is the half of the court where your team's offensive basket is located.

3. _____ Personal fouls are the only type of fouls that are never penalized with a free throw.

4. _____ It is impossible for a team that makes fewer field goals than its opponent to win the game.

5. _____ A player who establishes defensive position, and jumps straight up with arms directly overhead should not be called for blocking.

6. _____ Guards are usually most comfortable playing on the blocks.

7. _____ A 5-second violation cannot be called if the inbounds passer calls a time-out between the fourth and fifth count.

8. _____ If neither team is in the bonus, a personal (non-shooting) foul by either team would result in the ball being taken out of bounds.

9. _____ The player who is least likely to turn the ball over should be positioned as small forward.

10. _____ Basketball is an easier sport to teach than most because kids typically know the fundamentals.

Answers: 1. F, 2. T, 3. F, 4. F, 5. T, 6. F, 7. F, 8. T, 9. F, 10. F

Unit 7

What Basketball Skills and Drills Should I Teach?

In unit 4 you learned how to teach basketball skills and plan for practices. Now it's time to consider exactly what basketball skills to emphasize and what activities you'll use to help your players develop them. In this unit we'll describe the basic skills and recommend a variety of drills you can use to develop your players' basketball skills.

What Basketball Skills Are Important?

This section describes the basic basketball skills you'll want your players to learn during the season. Remember, start with the most basic individual skills and slowly progress players through more difficult techniques. Monitor players' understanding of each new skill by asking them specific questions about the skill and watching them attempt to perform it. Then you won't lose them along the way as you advance your skill instruction.

The following symbols will be used in figures throughout the remainder of the book to represent players, their movements, and the skills they are performing:

Defensive player	✕
Offensive player	◯
Ball location	●
Path of player	⟶
Path of pass	----▶
Path of dribble	∿▶
Screen	⊢

In addition, to help you select which drills match the skill level of your players, we've labeled every drill with either a **B** for beginner, **I** for intermediate, or **A** for advanced.

Position and Movement

Many coaches take for granted their players' ability to position and move around the court. Don't! You'll save a lot of time and increase your players' effectiveness if you emphasize proper footwork in every one of your practices.

Ready Position

The most basic basketball position is the ready position. Instruct your players to stand relaxed with arms and legs bent, feet shoulder width apart, and weight shifted slightly forward to the balls of the feet (see Figure 7.1). From this position a player can run forward or backward, slide to either side, cut, pivot, and jump. So, from the very first practice, have your players assume and maintain an alert ready position on the court.

■ **Figure 7.1** Ready position.

Stopping

One of the most common violations that beginners experience is traveling, usually due to poor stopping skills. Once you've explained the ready position, you'll want to help your players learn how to start and stop with their bodies under control. Young players need to learn the jump stop so they can stop after moving quickly either with or without the ball.

Jump Stop. Have players begin in the ready position, then blow your whistle and have them sprint forward five or six steps. When they hear your whistle the second time, have them stop quickly with both feet simultaneously hitting the floor, landing in a balanced, ready position. By using the jump stop, players are able to gather and control their forward momentum and may use either foot as a pivot foot for offensive moves. Practice this simple stop often. Until beginning players learn how to control their momentum, either with or without the ball, they will be playing out of control.

Pivots, Cuts, and Slides

After players have mastered the jump stop, you'll want to help them with some other basic footwork:

- turning or pivoting on either foot to change direction.
- pushing off either foot when running to cut quickly.
- sliding their feet on defense without crossing them.

Pivots. Along with helping your players to master the ready position and the jump stop, helping them to pivot correctly will give them a lot of confidence in their footwork.

A pivot simply involves stopping, then turning on one foot to move forward (front pivot) or dropping one foot backward (back pivot), all while keeping the ball of one foot on the court (see Figure 7.2).

Remind players that after using a jump stop they may choose either foot as their pivot foot, but they may not change that pivot foot while in possession of the ball. Each time they receive the ball, they should assume the ready position, and then they may use their pivot foot to

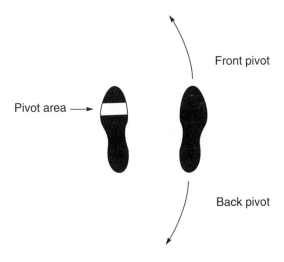

Pivot area →

Front pivot

Back pivot

■ **Figure 7.2** One-foot pivot.

- pivot to protect the ball from the defense,
- pivot to pass to a teammate, or
- pivot to make a move to the basket.

Cuts. The ability to change direction quickly and in balance is important on both the offensive and the defensive end of the court. Offensive players will have trouble getting open for passes or shots if they cannot "lose" their opponents with quick cuts. Defenders will find it difficult to keep up with effective offensive players if they are unable to respond to various cuts.

Therefore, teach your players how to cut on the court by having them practice planting one foot on the court at the end of a stride, then pushing off that foot to shift their momentum in another direction. For example, tell players to push off with the left foot if they wish to cut to the right. Then they should turn the unplanted foot in the direction they want to go and lead with that leg as they burst toward the new direction. When cutting, players should learn to bend their knees to lower their center of gravity and provide explosiveness to their legs. Effective cuts are hard, sharp, and explosive. Three very effective cuts used by offensive players to get open are the L-cut, V-cut, and backdoor cut (see Figure 7.3).

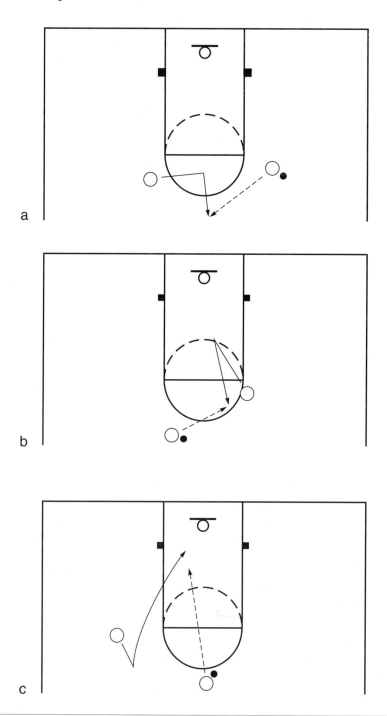

■ **Figure 7.3** (a) L-cut, (b) V-cut, and (c) backdoor cut.

Error Detection and Correction for Pivoting

Young players are often unsure of how to move or turn without using the dribble when they have the basketball. Therefore, they need help in learning how to pivot with the ball.

ERROR: Moving and switching the pivot foot while in possession of the ball

CORRECTION

1. Teach players to use the jump stop so they can use either foot to pivot on (see Figure 7.4).

2. Teach players to pivot away from the defensive pressure and square up to face the basket as soon as they receive the ball.

3. Remind players that once they choose a pivot foot, they cannot lift that foot from or slide it across the floor.

4. Encourage players to take full advantage of their ability to pivot in either direction as long as they keep the ball of the pivot foot in the same spot.

■ **Figure 7.4** Pivot toward the basket.

Slides. Basketball defenders must be able to slide their feet and maintain an arm's distance from their opponent who is attempting to drive or cut to the basket. But youngsters are much more comfortable with forward than with lateral movement and thus tend to cross their feet when attempting to move sideways. Therefore, you will need to take time to teach and drill them to slide their feet effectively.

Instruct players to stand in the ready position and then move the leg nearest their intended direction about 2 feet to that side. Next they should slide the other foot until the feet once again are shoulder-width apart (see Figure 7.5). Remind players to keep their toes pointed forward and to move as quickly as possible on the balls of their feet. They'll be able to slide more quickly if they keep their knees bent, rears down, and backs erect.

■ **Figure 7.5**   Lateral slides.

Pivot, Cut, and Slide Drills

Name.   Catch and Pivot (B)

Purpose.   To help players learn to move the ball effectively and pivot toward the basket as soon as they catch the ball

Organization.   Eight players are at each end of the court with one ball. Players form a box with two players in line at each corner of the box. One player starts on the block, another player is at the side of the free throw line, another player is at the free throw line extended out at the wing, and finally a player with the ball is on the baseline extended out from the block. A second player stands behind each of these four players. Passing begins counterclockwise with the first player in line stepping up to receive the next pass, pivoting away from the basket and passing to the next spot in the box. After passing, players follow the pass to the end of the line they passed to (see Figure 7.6). After 2 minutes reverse the direction of the passes and pivots.

Coaching Points. Look for good, crisp passing and quick pivots. See that players don't switch their pivot feet. Remind players to stay in ready position on balance when cutting, pivoting, and passing. Have players switch sides of the court after 3 minutes. This drill also works well as a pregame warm-up.

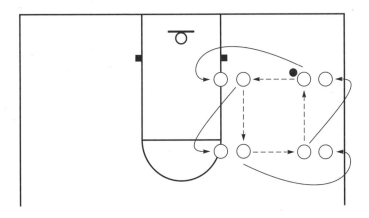

■ **Figure 7.6** Catch and Pivot Drill.

Name. V-Cut and Layup (I)

Purpose. To teach players how to cut and get open and how to convert layups when they are open

Organization. Six players are at each end of the court, three players on each wing. A coach is positioned at the top of the key at each end of the court and directs the drill as follows. The first player in each line has a ball and passes to the coach, then V-cuts and receives a return pass. After receiving the pass, the player pivots to face the hoop, then dribbles with the outside hand to the basket and shoots a layup. When the player begins the dribble to the basket, the player in the line on the opposite wing throws a pass to the coach and duplicates the movements of the first player. After shooting the layup, the player throws the ball to the first player in the opposite line and goes to the back of that line.

Coaching Points. Have players cut quickly, as if they are being guarded closely by a defender. Watch that they use proper catching and pivoting technique. Tell them to concentrate on driving hard to the hoop and shooting the layup correctly.

Variation. To help players understand why they are V-cutting (to get open!), you might put a stationary defensive player in front of each cutter. This will give the players an opportunity to V-cut and fake the defender out of position before receiving the pass. Have the defender react to a good V-cut, then stand passively as the player squares up to face the basket and drives.

Name. Lane Slide (B)

Purpose. To improve lateral movement and footwork

Organization. Two players are assigned to each free throw lane. One player has the ball at the free throw line. The other player in the pair is positioned on a block. The player with the ball rolls it to the block opposite the partner. The partner slides across the lane, retrieves the ball, and fires a quick chest pass to the player at the line. Upon receiving the return pass, the player at the free throw line rolls the ball to the opposite block, and the partner slides over to retrieve it. This sequence is repeated until the player on the block has retrieved and returned 10 passes. Then the players switch positions and repeat the drill.

Coaching Points. Watch that the player on the block slides across the lane without crossing the feet. The player should maintain the ready position throughout the drill, staying low with the head up. Emphasize good, crisp passes back to the partner at the free throw line.

Ballhandling Skills

A key to success in basketball is moving the ball effectively into position to take high-percentage shots. Therefore the skills of passing, catching, dribbling, and shooting are essential to success in basketball.

Passing

Passing is an offensive skill used to maintain possession and create scoring opportunities. Passes should usually be short and crisp, because long or slow passes are likely to be stolen by an opposing player. However, players should avoid throwing too hard or using passes that are difficult to control. Players should pass the ball above the waist and within easy reach of the receiver. If possible, passes should be thrown to the receiver's side that is farthest from her or his defender. As your players become more skilled, work with them on faking a pass one way, then passing another.

Keep it simple at the beginning by starting your players with these four types of passes:

- Chest pass
- Bounce pass
- Two-hand overhead pass
- One-hand bounce pass

Chest Pass. An often overlooked element of good passing is how to use the legs to generate the momentum for a pass. Begin by teaching your players to start in ready position and always to step toward their target to initiate the pass. The chest pass, shown in Figure 7.7, is so named because the ball is thrown with two hands from the passer's chest to the receiver's chest area. Teach your players to throw the pass with their thumbs snapping down and together.

■ **Figure 7.7**   Chest pass.

Bounce Pass.   Sometimes it is easier for a passer to get the ball to a teammate by bouncing the ball once on the court before it reaches the receiver. For example, a defender may be guarding a player with both hands overhead, preventing a pass through the air to a teammate. In that case a bounce pass may be the only route to get the ball to a teammate. Instruct your players to use bounce passes when they are closely guarded and may not have the space to extend their arms in a chest pass.

Teach players to bounce the ball on the court two-thirds of the way between themselves and the receiver, as illustrated in Figure 7.8. Remind them to use their legs and to step toward the target. Snapping their thumbs down and together as they release the pass will give the ball some backspin. Backspin will slow the pass down a little as it hits the floor and give the receiver a chance to catch the ball at waist level in ready position.

■ **Figure 7.8** Bounce pass.

Two-Hand Overhead Pass.   Another pass option is the two-hand overhead pass. This pass is often a good way for a guard to get the ball in to a center or forward in the lane. It also is useful for throwing an outlet pass to a teammate on a fast break.

The pass must be thrown with a hand on each side of the ball, with the thumbs behind the ball. The ball should not be brought back too far behind the head, or it becomes vulnerable to the defense. The passer must generate momentum toward the target by stepping first with the legs and following through with both arms extended (see Figure 7.9). Tell your players to aim for the receiver's head, because that's where the receiver wants to catch the ball, just above the head.

■ **Figure 7.9** Two-hand overhead pass.

One-Hand Bounce Pass. This is a good pass for beginners to learn as they try to combine their pivoting and passing skills. A player who is closely guarded may not have room to fully extend and make a crisp chest, bounce, or overhead pass. Thus the one-hand bounce pass allows a closely guarded player to pivot and step around the defense, bouncing the pass to a teammate with one hand, the other hand protecting the ball from the defense. The one-hand bounce pass is a quick, short, crisp pass used to get the ball to a cutting teammate. Beginners and advanced players alike may use this pass effectively to pass around pesky defenders.

Catching

Even the best passes are of little value if they aren't caught. Sloppy receiving technique is often the cause of turnovers and missed scoring opportunities. Emphasize the following receiving techniques:

- Show a target to the passer and call for the ball.
- Move to meet the pass, step toward the ball—not away.
- Watch the ball into the hands.
- Use two hands, palms facing the passer, thumbs together.

In most situations after receiving a pass, players should come to a jump stop with their feet positioned shoulder-width apart in ready position. From this position, players should pivot to face the basket, looking for an open teammate, a shot, or a lane to dribble the ball to the basket. Catching passes on fast breaks is more difficult because a player's momentum will be moving toward the basket, not toward the pass. Stress to your players the importance of providing a target and being alert for a pass on a fast break. Catching a pass while moving at full speed (without traveling) is very challenging for novice players. Emphasize visual and verbal contact with the passer and providing a good target. These cues will help receivers prepare for the pass and stay in control after they catch it.

Passing and Catching Drills

Name. Partner Passing (B)

Purpose. To help players learn to pass and catch properly

Organization. Have players pair up facing each other between the free throw lane lines. Each partner set has a ball. The pairs begin chest-passing the ball accurately and quickly to one another.

Coaching Points. Emphasize making quick passes and using proper receiving techniques. Be sure your players are using correct footwork, giving targets, calling for the ball, and using their legs to generate momentum for each pass.

Variations:

Partner Passing–Bounce Pass (B). Same drill, except players bounce-pass the ball.

Partner Passing–Overhead Pass (B). Same drill, except players throw overhead passes.

Name. Shotgun Passing (I)

Purpose. To teach players to use their peripheral vision when passing and catching so they can see the entire floor and still make quick and accurate passes

Organization. Six players are at each end of the court. In each group, one player stands with a ball at the free throw line, facing away from the basket. The other five players position themselves in a semicircle from one side of the free throw line to the other, facing their teammate out front in the shotgun position. One player among the five in the semicircle has a basketball. The drill begins with the player in the shotgun throwing a chest pass to one of the four players in the semicircle who do not have a basketball. As soon as this pass is made, the player in the semicircle who began the drill with a ball chest-passes the ball to the shotgun (see Figure 7.10). This drill continues for 1 minute. Players then rotate clockwise so the player on the right side of the free throw line moves to the shotgun position and the player in the shotgun moves to the left side of the free throw line.

Coaching Points. Emphasize quick and accurate passing. Timing is very important to the success of this drill. All players in the semicircle should have their targets (hands) up and be ready to receive a pass from the shotgun at any time. Shotguns must be alert for passes coming at them and make sure their passes are quick and accurate.

Variation. Shotgun Bounce (B). Same as above, except players bounce-pass the ball to one another.

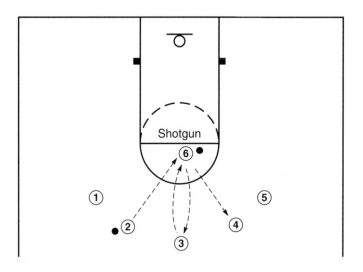

Figure 7.10 Shotgun Passing Drill.

Name. Monkey in the Middle (A)

Purpose. To improve players' ability to pass and pass-fake when guarded closely by a defender

Organization. Have four groups of three players spread out throughout the gym. Two offensive players in each group face each other, 10 to 12 feet apart. The third player is a defender (monkey in the middle), positioned between the offensive players, within 2 feet of the offensive player with the ball. One offensive player attempts to bounce- or chest-pass to a partner while the defender attempts to prevent the pass. Passers and receivers cannot move more than one step to either side, and passers cannot lob the ball over the defender's head. In fact, you may want to prohibit any overhead passes to encourage better faking and have your players concentrate on their bounce, chest, and one-hand bounce passes for this drill. After 20 seconds have all three players rotate one position so each player has a turn in the middle.

Coaching Points. Encourage offensive players to use fakes and read where the defender has his or her hands when attempting a pass. Make sure offensive players are not traveling and that the passes they make are catchable. Finally, prompt defenders to hustle and make the passers work hard to pass around them.

Dribbling

If there's one thing that young players like to do when they get their hands on a basketball, it's to bounce it. Unfortunately, when they practice on their own, only a few players dribble correctly or use techniques that will improve their dribbling skill. Therefore, you'll need to teach your players how to dribble effectively and watch that they use the correct dribbling technique as shown in Figure 7.11.

■ **Figure 7.11** Correct dribbling technique.

Teaching players correct dribbling technique is problematic, because most of them have already established incorrect dribbling habits. The three most common errors of self-taught youth dribblers are these: slapping at the ball from the chest area and waiting for it to bounce back up; keeping the head down, with eyes riveted to each bounce; and using one hand exclusively to bounce the ball.

As you correct these dribbling errors and attempt to improve your players' dribbling skills, advise them to

- establish a feel for the ball, with the pads of the fingers;
- maintain the ready position, keeping knees bent and rear down;

- keep the dribble under control and always bounce the ball below waist height, and even closer to the floor when being guarded closely;
- bounce the ball close to the body and protect the dribble from the defender with the non-dribbling hand and arm;
- keep the head up and see the rest of the court (and teammates!);
- learn how to dribble with the right and left hands; and
- keep practicing!

Dribbling Dos and Don'ts

Do . . .

- keep the dribble "alive" until you have a shot or an open teammate to pass to.
- vary the speed and direction of the dribble so defenders are kept off guard.
- protect the dribble from the defensive player with the non-dribbling arm when being closely guarded.
- cross-over or switch dribbling hands to protect the ball after dribbling past the defender.
- stay in the middle of the court and away from the sidelines and corners to avoid being trapped.

Don't . . .

- automatically start dribbling after receiving a pass. Look to see what shooting or passing options are available after squaring up to the basket.
- pick up or stop dribbling with no other option (shot or pass) available.
- dribble into a crowd—the ball is more likely to be stolen.
- try to get fancy when good fundamental dribbling will do the job.
- hesitate. Be assertive and confident when dribbling the ball.

Dribbling Drills

Name. Stationary Dribbling (B)

Purpose. To help players develop a feel for the ball and learn how to maintain control

Organization. Start with your players spread out facing you in two or three lines. Have them begin in ready position dribbling in place with their dominant (strong) hand while protecting the ball with their non-dominant (weak) hand. Move among the lines and check their balance, make sure their seats are down, backs straight and heads up (not watching the ball). When you shout "Change," have them cross the ball quickly over to their non-dominant hand and assume the same stationary position, protecting the ball with their dominant hand.

Coaching Points. Vary the amount of time between changes so players have less time to adjust and assume the correct dribbling position. Emphasize finger pad control and not watching the ball.

Variation. Have players go down on one knee while doing this drill. This forces them to dribble quickly and maintain control close to the floor.

Name. Leg Circles (I)

Purpose. To teach players to control the ball with both hands and to keep their eyes off the ball

Organization. Each player has a ball. Players spread out so that each has a 3-foot radius of clear space in which to dribble. Players should all face the same direction, with the coach in front of them. The players dribble the balls around one leg at a time, using the right hand to dribble around the right leg and the left hand to dribble around the left leg. When they have dribbled this pattern in one direction successfully for 1 minute, have them switch directions and dribble the same pattern for another minute.

Coaching Points. Test players for keeping their heads up while dribbling by raising a certain number of fingers three times during each half of the drill. At the end of the first minute ask players what the three numbers were, and do the same for the second minute. Observe players' dribbling technique, making sure that they are keeping the ball close to the floor dribbling on their finger pads, and not slapping at the ball.

Variation. Monkey Drill (A). Organize players as described, but have players control the ball by dribbling it between their legs in this sequence: right hand in front of legs, left hand in front of legs, right hand behind legs, left hand behind legs, and return to right hand in front of legs to start sequence again (see Figure 7.12).

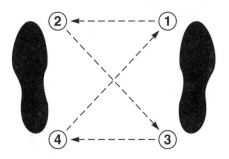

■ **Figure 7.12** Monkey Drill.

Name. Whistle Dribble (B)

Purpose. To practice changing direction quickly and looking up while dribbling

Organization. Each player has a ball. Players spread out in the middle part of the court, all facing the coach in the same direction. Use a whistle to have them start dribbling. When the coach points right and blows the whistle again, they should dribble hard with their right hand to the right. When the coach blows the whistle again, they should cross over to their left hand and dribble hard to their left. Players should always face the coach, who points in the direction players are to dribble.

Coaching Points. Keep players guessing by varying the direction. Have players dribble with the right hand when going right, and with the left hand when going left. Remind players to keep their heads up and to dribble low to the floor, especially when switching hands with the dribble.

Variation. Whistle Jump (B). Same drill, but whenever the whistle blows twice in succession, players should grip the ball with both hands and come to a two-foot jump stop in the ready position, ready to dribble in either direction the coach points.

Shooting

Every player loves to put the basketball through the hoop. So your players will be highly motivated to learn proper shooting technique if you convince them that it will help them make more of their shots.

To get the fundamentals of shooting across and encourage your players to learn them, tell them they'll SCORE if they do these things:

S—Select only high-percentage shots.

C—Concentrate on their target.

O—Order movements: square up, bend knees and elbows, cock wrist.

R—Release and wave "good-bye" to the ball.

E—Extend the shooting arm up and out toward the basket.

Players can shoot the ball in a variety of ways, including jump shots, set shots, free throws, and layups. Introduce your team to each variation, and emphasize the shots that they are most capable of executing at their stage of development.

Jump and Set Shots. Although the most common shot at higher levels of play is the jump shot, young players who lack the leg strength and coordination to spring from the floor while shooting will more often shoot set shots. So teach your players the mechanics of the set shot first, and they will be able to advance to the jump shot as they increase strength and improve coordination.

Teach your players these shooting mechanics in this sequence:

1. Lay the ball on the finger pads of each hand, with the shooting hand behind and slightly underneath the ball and the non-shooting hand balancing the ball from the side.

2. Focus on a specific target, usually the rim or backboard. The middle of the rim should be the target for most shots, but when at a 30- to 60-degree angle from the hoop, sight the corner of the square on the backboard for a bankshot (see Figure 7.13).

3. Align shoulders, hips, and feet square with (facing) the basket. The foot on the shooting-hand side can be up to 6 inches in front of the other foot so that the base of support is comfortable and balanced.

4. Bend the knees to get momentum for the shot. Let the legs, not the arms, be the primary power source for the shot.

■ **Figure 7.13** Sighting the basket.

5. Bend the shooting-arm elbow to approximately a 90-degree angle, keeping the forearm perpendicular to the floor and in front of the cocked wrist as the ball is brought up to the shooting position above the forehead (see Figure 7.14).

6. As the legs are extended, release the ball by extending the elbow, bringing the wrist forward, and moving the fingers of the shooting hand up and through the ball (see Figure 7.15). The non-shooting arm and hand should maintain their supportive position on the side of the ball until after the release.

7. Follow through after the release by landing on both feet, extending the shooting arm and dropping the wrist, pointing the index finger of the shooting hand directly at the basket.

For several practices your players will probably have difficulty shooting the ball properly. That's because they've developed bad shooting habits, and the correct shooting motion is awkward for them. Check that your players aren't shooting "line drives" at the hoop. Help them to see how important proper arc is in allowing the shot a reasonable chance to go in. Remind them to shoot the ball up, then out, toward the basket.

■ **Figure 7.14**   Correct stance for the set shot.

■ **Figure 7.15**   Proper ball release on the set shot.

Error Detection and Correction for Shooting

Many kids take a dribble before every shot. This is a bad habit because it allows the defense to recover and prevent, pressure, or block the shot. So you'll want to break them of this habit and get them to shoot without putting the ball on the floor.

ERROR: Dribbling before shooting when open, within good shooting range, or without a clear path to the basket

CORRECTION

1. Receive the pass and pivot to face the basket in the ready position.
2. Hold the ball in preparation for a shot or a two-handed pass.
3. Check where the defense is positioned, whether a shot is open and whether a teammate closer to the basket is open (see Figure 7.16).
4. If the nearest defender does not deny the shot and no teammate is open for a higher percentage shot, shoot the ball.

■ **Figure 7.16** Check possible options before shooting.

Free Throws. After shooting fouls, and when the team is in the bonus, the player fouled is awarded free throws. The free throw is nothing more than an uncontested set shot from a designated spot–the free throw line. Players should use the same shooting mechanics outlined for the jump and set shots. However, because free throw attempts are unhurried and uncontested, teach players to take a deep breath and take their time before shooting. Encourage them to think positive thoughts (e.g., "This one's in.") or visualize their shot falling through the net. These positive affirmations, along with proper form, will help your players take advantage of their trips to the line.

Layups. The highest percentage shot, and therefore the most desirable shot, is a layup. However, with young and inexperienced players, layups are hardly "gimmies," so you'll need to work with your team on proper layup technique from both sides of the basket.

A layup is a one-handed shot taken within 3 feet of the basket (see Figure 7.17). Teach players to use their left hands when shooting layups from the left side of the basket and their right hands when shooting from the right side of the basket. The layup motion begins with the player planting and exploding (much like a high jumper) off the foot opposite the shooting hand, after striding from a 45° angle to the hoop. The player explodes off the planted foot straight up into the air. At the top of the jump, the player releases the ball by bringing the shooting hand, which is underneath the ball and near the shoulder, up toward the basket. As in the jump and set shots, the index finger of the shooting hand should be pointed directly at the basket or the appropriate spot on the backboard. Teach beginning players always to use the backboard on their layups. It gives them a steady target to aim for every time.

■ **Figure 7.17** Layup.

Your right-handed players are likely to find left-handed layups troublesome, just as your left-handed players are going to find right-handed layups difficult. Point out to them the reason for using the hand farthest from the basket to shoot the ball: The ball is more easily protected and less easily blocked. Then "walk" them through the proper footwork taking one step with their left foot and exploding up to shoot with no dribble on the right side. Then have them back up and step with their right, then left and shoot. Finally have them back up and dribble *once*, stepping right, then left and shooting. Repeat this walk through (no dribble) sequence on the left side. Once they get the mechanics down without worrying about dribbling, they can speed up their approach and add the drive.

Shooting Drills

Name. Lay-In Stay In (B)

Purpose. To get players to concentrate and use correct layup technique when shooting close to the basket

Organization. Players are divided into two equal lines, one on each side of the lane, facing the basket, with the first player in each line one dribble away from the hoop. The first two players in one line each have a basketball. The first player with a ball goes in and shoots a layup while the first player in the opposite line goes in to rebound. The second player in the shooting line with a ball dribbles once to the hoop just as the first shooter begins to shoot. The player who rebounds the first shot passes the ball to the third player in the shooting line who is moving toward the basket. Players alternate between the rebounding and shooting lines. Switch the shooting line to the opposite side of the court after 5 baskets are made.

Coaching Points. Look for proper technique. Encourage players always to use the backboard, jump straight up, and protect the ball with their non-shooting hand.

Name. Around the World (I)

Purpose. To improve shooting skill from various spots on the court and shooting without dribbling

Organization. Assign three players to each hoop. Each group should have two basketballs. Two players in the group, each with a basketball, should be positioned near, but on opposite sides of the basket. These players serve as rebounders (R) for the third teammate, who shoots 10 consecutive shots from five designated spots that form a semicircle in front of the backboard. Beginning from a spot on the baseline 8 to 10 feet from the basket, the shooter catches a pass from one of the rebounders and shoots a shot. The shooter then hustles to the next spot, calls for the ball and gives a target, receives a pass from the other rebounder, and goes up for another shot. By this time, the rebounder who threw the first pass will have retrieved the ball and can deliver a pass to the shooter, who has moved to the third spot on the floor, near the middle of the free throw line. This sequence continues until the shooter has shot from each of the five spots twice (see Figure 7.18). Then one of the rebounders takes the shooter's position and the shooter becomes a rebounder.

Coaching Points. Emphasize hustling from one shooting position to the next. Check that shooters are using proper footwork and shooting form. Passes by the rebounders need to be accurate and timely.

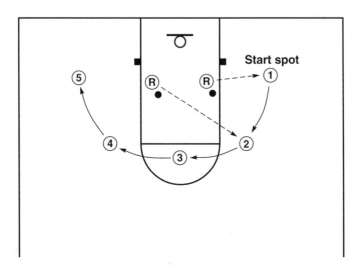

■ **Figure 7.18** Around the World Drill.

Defensive Skills

The individual defensive skills of basketball are sometimes less appreciated than the individual offensive techniques, but they are just as important. Kids need to learn the basics of player-to-player defense from the outset if they are to compete successfully in drills, scrimmages, and games.

Moving the Feet

From the ready position, described on page 77, a defender can move quickly in any direction and maintain balance. Have your players practice sliding in short, quick, lateral bursts (as described on page 82) from one point to another, without crossing their feet.

When an offensive player has gained an advantage by moving past the defender, the defender should turn and sprint to catch up and reestablish position. Even the best defensive players get beat momentarily. Emphasize to your players to keep their feet active on defense and not to reach and get off balance. If they do get beat by an offensive player, they should hustle back into position.

Guarding an Opponent With the Ball

Obviously, the reason for guarding offensive players with the ball is to prevent them from scoring. A defender can best accomplish this by staying between his or her assigned opponent and the basket. Trying to maintain an arm's distance from the offensive player with the ball is a good rule of thumb.

Tell your players to consider these things about their bodies and court positions when guarding a player with the ball:

- Body position
  - *Am I in ready position and alert?*
  - *Am I arm's distance from my player with the ball and able to put pressure on his/her ability to shoot, pass, or drive?*
  - *Am I aware that my player is predominately left- or right-handed so I can position my body to encourage him or her to use their weaker hand on a drive?*
- Court position
  - *Is my player close enough to attempt a good shot?*

> – *Am I close enough to the player to prevent an easy shot?*
> – *Am I too close, so the opponent can drive around me?*
> – *Will a teammate be able to help me if the player beats me with the dribble?*

Have your players focus on their opponent's mid-section. If defenders watch the ball or their opponent's head or feet, they are likely to react to a fake that will put them out of defensive position. As the offensive player begins to dribble, the defender should react by sliding the feet and maintaining an arm's distance from the opponent, trying to beat the offensive player to the spot that the player wants to reach. If the defender can get the offensive player to stop and pick up the ball, the defender can then move closer and crowd the offensive player by blocking the passing lanes, applying extensive pressure with the arms.

Guarding an Opponent Away From the Ball

Defending an opponent without the ball is just as important as guarding a player with the ball, but it is a bit more complicated. Whether an opponent is just one pass away from the ball, or as many as two passes away, defensive players need to learn the defensive concept of ball-player-self (see Figure 7.19). Defenders want to position themselves so they can see the ball (and know if they need to come and help a teammate on a pass or drive), and they must keep track of a moving opponent (their player) who may be trying to get open to receive a pass, or who may be setting a screen to free another teammate.

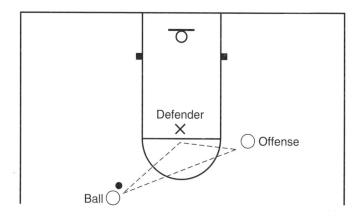

■ **Figure 7.19** Defending player without the ball (ball-player-self).

Error Detection and Correction for Guarding Away From the Ball

Too often, defensive players lose track of where their assigned offensive player is on the court. This happens because they're watching only the movement of the ball, not their player. You'll need to teach players how to position themselves so they can see both the player they are guarding and the ball.

ERROR: Defenders away from the ball losing track of where their offensive player is on the court

CORRECTION

1. Position players to see the ball and their player without turning their head (see Open Position on page 105).
2. Establish and maintain the ball-player-self relationship.
3. Have players point at the ball with one hand and their player with the other.
4. Players must adjust positions as the offensive player or ball changes position.
5. A player two or more passes away needs to be alert to help out on a drive or deflect a long pass attempt to their opponent in the corner (see Figure 7.20).

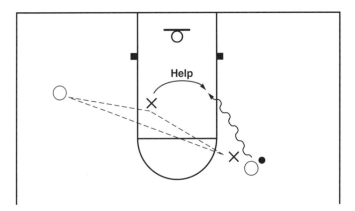

■ **Figure 7.20**   Defense away from the ball.

Denial Position.   Teach your players the denial position when their opponent is one pass away from the ball. The space between two offensive players where a pass can be made is called the *passing lane*. A defender wants to have an arm and leg in the passing lane when guarding a player who is one pass away (see Figure 7.21). This denial position allows the defender to establish the ball-player-self relationship and discourages the offensive player with the ball from even attempting a pass.

■ **Figure 7.21**   Denial position.

Open Position.   When offensive players are two or more passes away from the ball, the defensive player wants to establish an *open position* that still maintains the ball-player-self relationship. In the open position the defender is farther away from the offensive player, pointing to the ball with one hand, and the opponent with the other hand (see Figure 7.22). Using peripheral vision, the defender moves to react as the ball penetrates toward the basket (to help out on the drive) or into denial position if the offensive player cuts hard to receive a pass. In both the denial and open positions, the key is remembering always to maintain the ball-player-self relationship.

■ **Figure 7.22** Open position.

Defensive Drills

Name. Zigzag (B)

Purpose. To improve footwork when guarding dribblers

Organization. Have players pair up on the baseline, with two pairs in each of three lines. One player in each pair has a basketball and dribbles the length of the court in a zigzag pattern while the partner tries to move with the dribbler (see Figure 7.23). Have players switch roles when the dribbler reaches the opposite end of the court.

Coaching Points. Have defenders work on their footwork and staying in the ready position, arm's distance from the dribbler. Warn them not to reach for the ball and to concentrate on staying slightly ahead of the dribbler. Tell dribblers not to race downcourt, but to take three controlled dribbles in one direction before changing direction. They should dribble under control, from one side to the other, dribbling with the hand on the side of the direction they are moving, and protecting the ball from the defender.

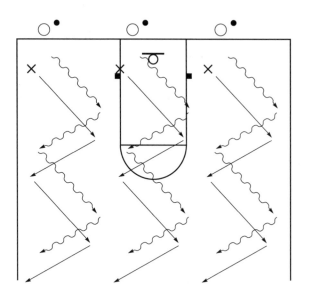

■ **Figure 7.23** Zigzag Drill.

Name. Cut the Cutter (I)

Purpose. To practice defending against players who are working hard to get open

Organization. Two passers are at the top of the key with passer #1 holding the ball. One offensive player is on the block guarded by a defensive player. The offensive player breaks out of the wing (10–15 feet), and the defensive player sprints out to deny the pass. The offensive player cuts back toward the block, and the defense reacts by staying in denial position with one hand and leg in the passing lane. Passer #1 then passes across to passer #2 (see Figure 7.24a), and the defense adjusts to the new location of the ball by opening up (two passes away now) and getting off the offensive player who is still on the far side block. When all the adjustments have been made by the defense, passer #2 slaps the ball and the offensive player cuts through the lane directly toward the ball, with the defender reacting and denying the cut (see Figure 7.24b). When the offensive player gets to the top of the key, passer #2 throws the pass, and the defender should be able to knock it away with the denial hand/arm.

Coaching Points. Emphasize denying the ball with an arm and leg in the passing lane, using peripheral vision to see the ball and the cutter in the open position, beating the cutter to the spot, and proper defensive footwork to recover into the ready position if the offense does receive the pass.

Variation. Same drill except on the last cut to the top of the key, the defense denies, but allows the offense to catch the ball, then recovers to ready position (on ball) to play one-on-one against the offense.

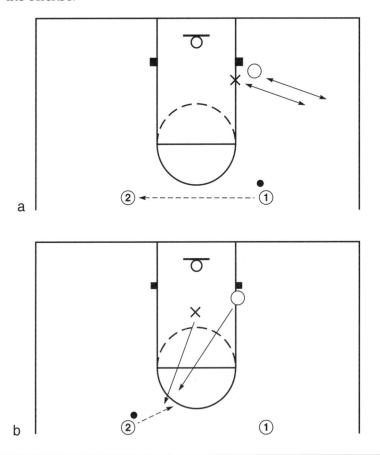

■ **Figure 7.24** Cut the Cutter Drill.

Rebounding

Rebounding, or gaining possession of a missed shot, is both an offensive and a defensive skill.

When a shot is taken, players should not simply stand and watch to see whether it goes in or not. You must get your players in the habit of positioning themselves advantageously for rebounds. They should react immediately by "boxing out," getting between the opposing player and the basket and putting their rear in contact with the opponent's body (see Figure 7.25). Players may use a front or rear pivot to turn and box out their opponent. A front pivot allows the defense to turn while watching the offense move toward the rebound. A rear pivot is used to move into the path of the offense without the same visual contact. Encourage defenders to use whichever method gets them in position in front of the offense, sealing the offensive player away from the basket.

■ **Figure 7.25** Boxing out.

You must warn your players to avoid reaching over an opponent when they get boxed out. They'll get called for a foul if they do. Emphasize the importance of jumping straight up for the rebound. Not only will a vertical jump achieve greater height, but players will avoid needless fouls if they go straight up.

Here are some additional rebounding tips you'll want to share with your players:

- A shot taken from the side is very likely to rebound to the opposite side of the basket. Therefore, players should try to get position on the opposite side of the basket when such a shot is taken.

- Once contact is established, the defensive rebounder wants to maintain that contact until releasing to jump for the rebound.

- After controlling a rebound, players should keep the ball at chin level with their elbows out (see Figure 7.26).

■ **Figure 7.26** Proper position after rebound.

Rebounding Drills

Name. Sky and Score (B)

Purpose. To improve the timing for offensive rebounding

Organization. One line of offensive rebounders is at the free throw line. The coach is at the top of the key with the ball. The coach takes a shot which hits off the backboard. The first player in line moves in from the free throw line to get the rebound and goes right back up and scores.

Coaching Points. Vary the rebound so players must watch where the ball hits and anticipate when they should jump to catch the ball at the top of their jump. Remind players to land on balance after securing the rebound and keep the ball at chin level with their elbows out.

Name. Glass Cleaner (I)

Purpose. To teach boxing out technique and outlet passing

Organization. One line is at the top of the key. The first two players move down into the lane, while the third player moves out to an outlet position. The coach is at the free throw line with the ball. The first player in the pair (closest to basket) faces the coach with the ball at the free throw line. This player is defense and will box out the offense on the shot. The coach shoots, the defensive rebounder calls "Shot!" and pivots to box out the offensive player (second player). The rebounder secures the ball and pivots to the outside to throw a crisp, two-hand overhead pass to the outlet, who calls for the ball while giving a target. The outlet passes to the coach, and moves to the end of the line at the top of the key. The offensive player steps down to face the coach and becomes the new defender. The defensive rebounder moves out to become the next outlet. The next person in line at the top of the key moves down to become the offensive player.

Coaching Points. The rebounder calls "Shot!" and pivots quickly to initiate the contact with the offense. The outlet calls for the ball and gives a target. Make sure the rebounder pivots away from the opponent and keeps the ball chin high to make the outlet pass.

How Do I Use Basketball Drills Effectively?

Now you know how to teach the basic individual skills of basketball, but you're probably wondering which drills to use to develop these skills in your players. Before jumping right into the drills, you should consider how you are going to set up your practice sessions to make such activities productive and efficient.

Throughout this unit, basketball drills have been outlined for each skill. When organizing your team for drills, maximize your use of court space to keep as many players active as possible. If you have 12 players on your team and four baskets, try to divide up into groups of three for many of your drills. And rather than having 5-on-5 scrimmages with two players sitting out, perhaps you can have two games of 3-on-3 going on simultaneously. Or, another option is to have 4-on-4 scrimmages, with the team that's sitting out practicing its offensive plays off to the side.

Here are some more tips for using basketball drills in practices:

- Help players understand how each drill will improve their skills and what is expected of them before letting them begin.

- Use individual and two-player drills frequently. These types of drills give each player more hands-on practice, and keeps all of them more active than do group drills.

- Use group drills only when the practice facility limits your alternatives (e.g., when there are only two baskets for a shooting drill), to practice teamwork, or to slow down the pace.

- Make sure players have ample space on the court. Assign players to particular baskets, sections of the court, rows, or any other type of arrangement that is best for the drill.

- Emphasize performance, not winning, when your players compete in drills. And be sure to match up players by skill and physical maturity to avoid lopsided competition.

- Explain drills thoroughly, but move quickly to demonstrating and then have players participate. Too much talking takes the fun and energy out of practice.

- Don't hesitate to stop a drill and make a correction that the whole group can benefit from. Repeated mistakes won't go away without your guidance.

Unit 8

How Do I Get My Players to Play as a Team?

To participate in games successfully, kids must not only develop the individual skills presented in unit 7, but must also understand and be able to execute team tactics. Therefore, in addition to the basic individual skills, you must teach your players the offensive and defensive team principles of basketball.

What About Team Offense?

In basketball, the offensive team's primary objective is to move the ball effectively so they can score. A secondary goal is to maintain ball possession so the opposing team cannot score. The following tactics will help your team accomplish these goals.

Offensive Team Principles

Purposeful and efficient movement is essential to the success of a basketball team's offense. Young players, however, have a strong tendency to stand around, watch the ball, and holler for the ballhandler to pass the ball to them. Because no one is open or moving to get open, the ballhandler–out of desperation–either puts up an ill-advised shot or tries to force a pass to a teammate. In either case, it's an unsuccessful possession, and the opposing team gets the ball.

Teach your players how to move with a purpose on offense:

- Keep the court balanced, so not everyone is on one side or the other.
- Penetrate the defense by driving or passing when possible.
- Set solid screens, and always roll to the basket.

Court Balance

A stationary player is easy to defend; so is an offensive team that is bunched together on the floor. That's why you'll want to teach and remind your players to spread out and balance the court on offense. When players are arranged in this manner, the path to the basket is less congested, and the defense is more susceptible to attack.

Penetration

One of the best ways for an offense to put pressure on the defense is to move the ball into the lane with a pass or dribble. Dribble penetration is effective when the ballhandler keeps the head up and maintains control of the ball. The dribbler can either shoot the ball or pass it to a teammate whose defender has left to stop the penetrator. Passes are the quickest means of penetration. Teach players to look for opportunities to penetrate.

If the offensive players force the ball into the "teeth" of the defense, they'll likely get called for charging or have the ball stolen, so make sure they penetrate under control.

Screens

Because young players often have difficulty getting open to receive or shoot the ball, you should teach them how to set screens for one another. An offensive player who sets a screen, or pick, positions himself or herself as a stationary barrier on one side of a teammate's defender; the idea is that the defender's path will be blocked as the teammate cuts around the screen to get open. The screening player stands erect with feet planted shoulder-width apart, keeping the arms down to the sides, or crossed at the chest.

Remind players that it does no good to set a screen for a ballhandler who has stopped dribbling. Direct them to "screen away" from the ball, meaning they should set screens for teammates who are on the opposite (weak) side of the court from the ball. That way the player for whom the screen is set will be moving toward the passer after coming off the screen. Also, even the best-set screens are worthless if the screen is not used effectively. So work with your players on setting up their opponents and then cutting right by (actually brushing by) the screeners.

Error Detection and Correction for Team Offensive Motion

Offensive players are easy to guard if they just stand in one place. So when you see your team standing around, direct them how and where to move effectively!

ERROR: Players all standing on one side of the court around the ballhandler shouting for the player to pass them the ball

CORRECTION

1. Players should spread out on the court (two of the players without the ball on one side, the other two on the opposite side). Keeping the floor balanced helps spread out the defense.

2. Players should V-cut or L-cut to get open, or help a teammate to get open by setting screens on or away from the ball (see Figure 8.1).

3. If the ballhandler has picked up the dribble, movements to get open must be even quicker and to a position where the passer can see the open player.

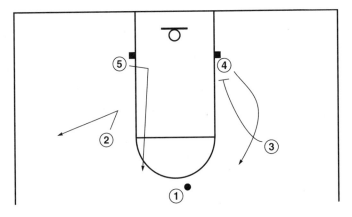

Figure 8.1 Motion offense.

Error Detection and Correction for Screening

Kids have trouble setting and using screens. Too often an offensive player is not patient enough and cuts before a screener has planted both feet. And just as often, the player setting the screen fails to set a solid screen so the teammate can use it to get open.

ERROR: Setting moving screens (which are illegal)

CORRECTION

1. Identify a teammate's defender to set a screen on.
2. Set the screen in a direction that allows the teammate using the screen to go to the basket or to the ball.
3. Plant both feet near the defender, facing the direction opposite where the teammate will cut.
4. Maintain the position until after the teammate has used the screen (see Figure 8.2).
5. Pivot or roll toward the ball.

■ **Figure 8.2** Legal screen.

General Team Patterns

Guard, forward, and center positions and their responsibilities were described in unit 6. Now let's look at how these players function within an offensive set. (For a diagram of positions #1 through #5, see Figure 6.3 on page 66.)

The #1 player must bring the ball up the court and initiate the offense. If the offense stalls in the hands of another player, the #1 player should go get the ball and start the offense again. Team organization, penetration, and defensive protection against fast breaks are among the primary concerns of the #1 position.

The #2 and #3 players should assist the #1 player with ballhandling duties when necessary. However, their primary concern should be to get open to receive a pass on the wings, preferably below the free throw line. Therefore, the #2 and #3 players should use screens set by the #4 and #5 players, V-cutting, L-cutting, and backdoor cutting as methods to get open.

The #4 and #5 players should remain in the lane area, in either the low-post (blocks) or high-post (free throw line) position. These players should get open by setting good, solid screens away from the ball. They should try to set screens for the #1, #2, and #3 players, then pivot and roll to the basket looking for a pass and layup. Although the #4 and #5 players must always be concerned about getting a 3-second violation, they should try to get open near the basket on the ball side of the court; and, when on the weak side, they should try to get in good rebounding position.

No matter what type of offense your team runs, these general instructions will help your players understand their roles on the team and their positions on the court. If you fail to effectively inform them, you'll find all five players grouped near the top of the key, standing around or getting in each other's way. Figure 8.3 illustrates the areas of the court in which the players typically run the offensive patterns just described.

Teamwork and Shot Selection

Even if your players do a great job of fulfilling their roles on offense, their efforts will all be for naught if they don't work together and take good shots. Although one player on the court makes up only 20% of the team, a lone "ballhog" or "gunner" can completely destroy the offense.

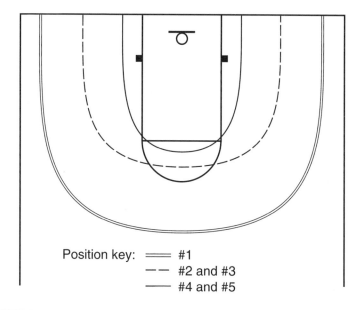

Position key: ═══ #1
━━ #2 and #3
──── #4 and #5

■ **Figure 8.3** Court areas for player positions.

Therefore, in practice make sure that everyone is involved in the offense and that players take the types of shots they will be taking during games. Remind your players to be patient, and give them confidence that their offense will open up scoring opportunities if they each do their part. Several good, crisp passes and solid screens should give your team a chance to score on every possession.

Special Situations

Inbounds, jump balls, free throws, and fast breaks are some of the special situations your team will need to be prepared for. Don't spend too much time on these aspects of the game because skill development needs a lot of practice time, but make certain that your players understand their roles when such situations arise.

Inbounds. Because youth leagues rarely allow pressing except for the last few minutes of the game, you need not devote practice time to inbounding the ball in the backcourt. Most of your inbound plays should be designed to create an easy scoring opportunity when your team puts the ball into play from underneath your basket. Keep the plays simple and few. Also, you might consider aligning in the same manner for each play, both so your players are not confused about where to position themselves and so the defense is not tipped off by a change in formation.

Two options for offensive inbounds are shown in Figure 8.4. But you can use your self-designed plays or those that you have learned from other coaches. The key is to have a good passer inbound the ball and for the rest of the team to cut hard to their designated spots.

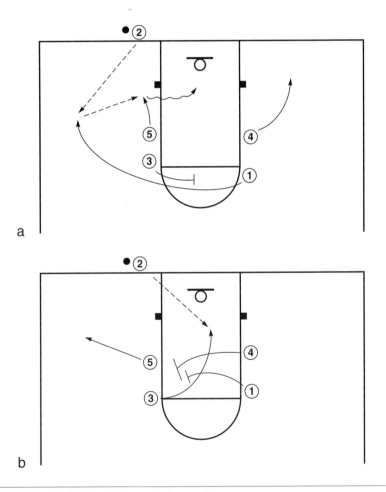

■ **Figure 8.4** Two inbound play options.

Jump Balls. The jump ball procedure was described in unit 6. However, you'll need to give your team some specific guidelines

for positioning themselves during games. How players are positioned should depend on whether your team or the opposing team
has the better chance of controlling the tip. If the player jumping for
you has an advantage, your team should align in an offensive formation and attempt to score off a play (see Figure 8.5a). But if it
appears that the opposing team will gain possession, a defensive
setup is appropriate (see Figure 8.5b).

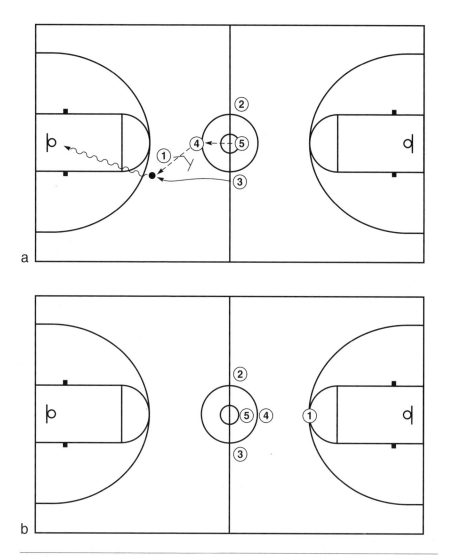

Figure 8.5 Jump ball formation for (a) offensive and (b) defensive tips.

Free Throws. The main things you need to remember about free throws are these:

- Have your best rebounders in the positions closest to the hoop.
- Remind players to block out the players next to them when the opposing team is shooting.
- Warn players about going over-the-back when the opponent has position in front of them.
- Designate a player to box out the shooter when the opposing team is shooting.
- Make certain one player is near midcourt when your team is shooting, to prevent easy fast breaks by the opposition.

Fast Breaks. If your team rebounds well and steals the ball often, you should teach your players the basics of executing the fast break. The following is a brief description of how to get your fast break started.

When a missed shot is grabbed, the rebounder must pivot toward the wing area on that side of the court, and hit the outlet (#1, #2, or #3) player. The player who receives the outlet pass should get the ball to the middle of the court with either the dribble or a pass to one of the better ballhandlers, usually #1, #2, or #3. Once the ball is at midcourt, the player with the ball should make sure that the two lanes on each side are filled before proceeding down the court. The players filling the lanes are sprinting down the court (ahead of the ballhandler if possible) and staying wide to spread out the retreating defenders. The player with the ball in the middle wants to get to the free throw line under control before passing to either lane for a shot or short drive. The last two players down the floor are called trailers (usually #4 and #5) and cut directly to the blocks on either side, looking for a pass from one of the outside lanes. Trailers often get passes on the blocks from the right or left lane cutters when the defense moves out to cover them on the wings. An example of the fast break is shown in Figure 8.6.

Offensive Team Drills

Name. Three-Player Weave (B/I)

Purpose. To help players improve their passing on the move, teamwork, and conversion of layup opportunities

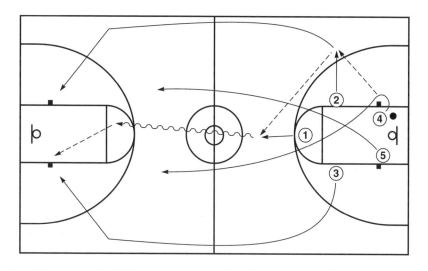

■ **Figure 8.6** Fast break.

Organization. Players are in three lines on one baseline, with the two outside lines just outside of the lane and the middle line centered with the basket. Each player in the middle line has a basketball. The first player in each line begins the drill. The middle player passes the ball to a player in one of the outside lines and runs behind that player. The player who received the pass moves quickly down toward the center of the court, passes the ball to the player who was in the opposite outside line, and runs behind that player. The player now with the ball makes a pass to the player who began the drill in the middle line and cuts behind that player while continuing to move downcourt. The same sequence continues until players near the opposite basket (see Figure 8.7). At that point, the first player to receive the ball close enough to shoot a layup without dribbling (or traveling) goes strong to the hoop and converts the basket. One player retrieves the ball, and the others move into position and begin the same passing weave to the other end of the court. As the layup is taken at the other end, the next three-player group begins passing and weaving the other way.

Coaching Points. Players love this drill and the teamwork involved if they don't get frustrated learning it. So walk them through it a couple of times to make sure they all get the hang of it. Emphasize crisp passes and players staying in tight as they pass and weave down the court. Also stress the importance of good communication while giving targets and calling for the ball.

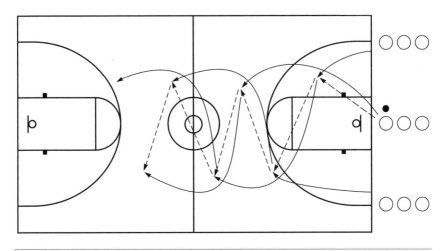

■ **Figure 8.7** Three-Player Weave Drill.

Name. Moving Triangle (I)

Purpose. To help players understand the pass and screen away concept

Organization. Position one player at the top of the key with a ball and one player on each block. Players on the blocks V-cut to get open at the wings at the same time. The top player passes to one side or the other, then goes away from the pass to screen the (imaginary) defender of the opposite wing. The player receiving the screen uses it to cut and get open for a return pass at the top of the key. Players continue to pass and screen away for five or six passes before looking to shoot off a pass.

Coaching Points. Emphasize that players V-cut to get open, wait for the screen to be set before cutting, and always square up to face the basket in ready position after receiving a pass.

Variation. Add defensive players and have all six first *walk* through the same pattern with the defense reacting to being either on the ball or off the ball. This may be one of the most valuable drills you can use with beginning players as they learn team offensive and defensive positioning.

Name.　Get It 'n Go (I)

Purpose.　To practice team rebounding and fast-breaking

Organization.　Five players are on the full-court with one ball. The coach shoots and #3, #4, and #5 position players should move to get the rebounds. The #1 and #2 players should move quickly to outlet positions as soon as a shot is taken. Five players run their fast break to the opposite end of the court.

Coaching Points.　Stress aggressive rebounding, proper outletting, and filling all the lanes on the fast break. Players will need to *walk* through this first and be reminded how important it is to communicate about which position they are taking.

Name.　3-on-2, 2-on-1 (A)

Purpose.　To teach the offensive players how to attack the basket when they outnumber the defense, especially on a fast break

Organization.　Have players form three lines behind one baseline. Each of the two outside lines should be midway between its sideline and its edge of the free throw lane. The third line is at the midpoint of the lane, with one player holding a ball. On the other end of the court, in tandem at the free throw line, are two defensive players. The first players in each line run downcourt passing the ball to one another. When the players reach midcourt, the ball goes to the player in the middle. This player must decide how to attack with the 3-on-2 advantage–whether to pass immediately to a teammate or to penetrate with the dribble until a defender stops them (see Figure 8.8). Teach the top defender to stop the dribbler and force the player to pass or pick up the dribble. Once a pass is made, the bottom defender (closest to the basket) should sprint out under control to defend the ball, and the top defender should drop quickly to prevent the opposite wing from getting a pass for a layup. If a pass is made back to the top and the shot is taken, the defenders box out and go after the rebound. They then become the offense and take the ball to the other end of the court while the player who was originally the middle player on offense hustles back to play defense 2 against 1. The players who were originally in the two outside lanes on offense remain on that end of the court while the 2-on-1 situation is played out on the opposite end of the court. These two players then serve as defenders against the next group to come down the court.

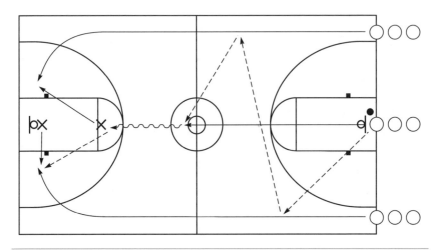

■ **Figure 8.8** 3-on-2, 2-on-1 Drill.

Coaching Points. Make the defenders stop penetration and force a
pass. In the 3-on-2 situation, have the middle player stop at the free
throw line and make a good pass to either wing. If you give your
players some guidelines to follow, they'll be more comfortable
taking advantage of their opportunities in these kinds of situations.

What About Team Defense?

Playing good defense involves using correct technique and working together with teammates. Because many youth leagues prohibit
zone defenses, and because the principles of solid player-to-player
defense can later be applied to teaching zones, this book does not
describe zone defense principles. The footwork fundamentals and
positioning techniques described in unit 7 are essential for all players on the team. And, as with offense, if but one player breaks down
on defense, the entire defense can collapse.

Defensive Team Principles

Emphasize to your players that proper individual techniques will make
them a strong defensive team. Praise them just as much for good defensive play as for scoring. Try to build players' desire to deny their

opponents the ball and to work as a unit. The following tactics, if performed successfully, will make your team a tough one to score on:

- Maintain position and balance.
- Cut off and deny the passing lanes.
- Handle screens and communicate.
- Help out.

Maintain Position and Balance

Young players often mistakenly attempt to steal the ball by swiping at it with their hands. Advise your players against such steal attempts because reaching will put them off balance, out of position, and in great jeopardy of being called for a foul. Therefore, encourage your players to play solid defense and refrain from risky steal attempts that can cause the entire defensive unit to break down.

Inexperienced players also need help judging the appropriate distance they should maintain from their offensive opponents. The closer your defenders are to the player with the ball, the more difficult it is for that player to pass and shoot. However, if defenders guard a player too closely–especially a player who has a quickness advantage–they are in danger of getting beat for an easy basket. So tell them to watch their opponent closely during the first few trips downcourt to determine how quick they are. Have them determine which hand the player shoots and dribbles with. Although this might seem a bit simplistic, advise your players to always be closer to the opponent's basket than are the players they are guarding (for an example, see Figure 8.9).

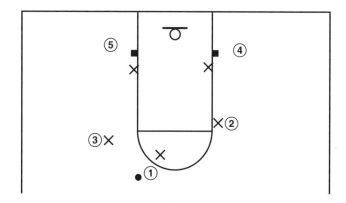

■ **Figure 8.9** Team defense player positions.

Cut Off the Passing Lanes

The best defensive teams make it difficult for the offense to dribble and pass, much less shoot the ball. Using the player-to-player defensive technique described in unit 7—forcing the opponents to use their weaker hand when dribbling—the player should be able to force opponents to pick up their dribble. However, preventing passes is sometimes more difficult.

The key to your players' denial of the opposition's passes is to have the off-ball defenders (those not guarding the ballhandler) maintain ball-player-self position (see Figure 8.10). Help your players learn to use their peripheral vision so they can see their player and the ball (without turning their heads) at all times. When the offense cuts toward the ball, good defenders try to beat them to the spot, and cut them off from receiving the pass. Playing good team defense means trying to prevent your opponent from ever receiving the ball!

It's not easy. Kids, and even pros, have difficulty cutting off the passing lanes. Help them adjust their positioning when their player is one or two passes away from the ball. They'll be a stronger defensive unit if they can understand this concept.

■ **Figure 8.10**　Ball-player-self position.

Error Detection and Correction for Defending Off the Ball

Even when they are in good position to cut off passes to the offensive players they are guarding, players need to be reminded which way to turn their bodies so they are best able to stick with the players to whom they are assigned.

ERROR: Defenders guarding players away from the ball, facing the ballhandler, or losing track of the player to which they are assigned

CORRECTION

1. Defenders should be in good open (see unit 7) position to cut off passes with their hand nearest the passer in the passing lane.

2. Every defender should be able to point to the player he or she is assigned as well as point to the location of the ball (as is the defender in Figure 8.11).

3. From the open position the defender should move to step into the passing lane and prevent the player from receiving a pass.

■ **Figure 8.11** Defender's open position off the ball.

Handle Screens and Communicate

Just as you will instruct your players to set screens to get open, so too will the opposing coach. Therefore, your players need to know how to handle screens.

First, defenders must learn to communicate with each other. They should be talking throughout each opponent's possession, shouting things like "Look out to the right, Pat!" "I've got your help over here!" "Take the ball, Terry!" When one of your players sees an opponent setting a screen on a teammate, he or she should immediately holler "Screen right!" or "Screen left!" and the name of the teammate being screened.

Figure 8.12 illustrates the three ways defenders can handle screens. The *over-the-top* approach should be used when the opponent who uses the screen leaves room for the defender to get around the screener. The defender on whom the screen was set should let the teammate know to stay with the screener by shouting "Over!" On the other hand, the player being screened should *hustle through* it if the teammate whose player is setting the screen leaves room behind the screen and if either defender shouts "Through!" Finally, the defenders should *switch* the players they are covering when the screener has done an effective job and there is no way that the defender who was screened can stay with the player who used the screen. In this case, the defender whose opponent set the screen should yell "Switch!" This is usually a last resort to all other ways of handling screens. By communicating, the defensive players let one another know what they are doing so the offense can't take advantage of their confusion.

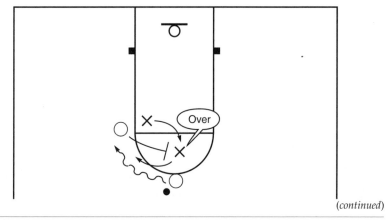

a

(continued)

■ **Figure 8.12** Defensive screens: (a) over-the-top, (b) hustle through, and (c) switch.

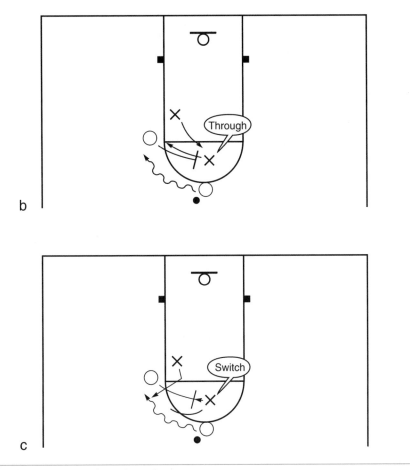

■ **Figure 8.12** *(continued)*

Help Out

No matter how well your players position themselves and communicate on defense, an offensive player will at times spring free. Therefore, you must instruct your players how to respond in these "help" situations.

Your instructions will vary depending on the type of help needed. For example, if one of your players spots an opponent wide open under the basket, waving for a teammate to pass the ball, that defender should leave an assigned opponent who is farther from the basket and sprint to try to prevent the pass. On the other hand, if a dribbler gets by a defender and is headed for a layup, the defensive player closest to the dribbler between the dribbler and the basket should immediately move in to cut off the lane to the hoop (see Figure 8.13). Whatever the case, the defender who has been beaten, or who loses an offensive player and sees that recovery is impossible, should shout "Help!" All four teammates should be ready to respond if you have effectively taught them this very important defensive tactic. Generally, you'll want your players to rotate toward the ball, with the closest defender coming to help first. The other four players must then rotate quickly to recover and pick up new players once the penetration has been stopped.

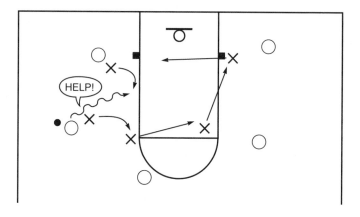

■ **Figure 8.13** Defensive help rotation.

■■■■■■■ **Defensive Team Drills** ■■■■■■■

Name. Screen Solution (B)

Purpose. To improve defenders' ability to react to and communicate about screens

Organization. Have players 3-on-3 at each end of the floor, with one ball at each end. Offensive players screen for the dribbler and away from the ball in no set pattern. Defenders call out and react to each screen and make the necessary adjustments. Teams alternate from offense to defense after each possession. Neither team is trying to score in this drill.

Coaching Points. Emphasize communication and handling screens on defense. See that offensive players set solid, stationary screens and that the teammate for whom the screen was set uses the screen effectively.

Name.   Weak-Side Help (A)

Purpose.   To practice defensive help reactions when a teammate gets beat by an offensive player

Organization.   Have players 3-on-3 on each half-court, with a coach at each end with a whistle. On every possession, the coach picks a moment to blow the whistle when an offensive player on the wing has the ball and is facing the basket. When the whistle is blown, the defender on that player allows the player to drive around to the basket. The player beaten should holler "Help!" and the nearest defender moves over to pick up the dribbler. The other two defenders move quickly to cover the two other offensive players (see Figure 8.14). Talk about who should provide the help and how the other two players should recover and adjust to their new assignments.

Coaching Points.   This is a great drill for working on all aspects of player-to-player defense, so watch that players maintain good ball-self-basket position and awareness when a teammate needs help. Emphasize swift response by the defense to the call for help. Because of its dynamic nature, this drill will teach players how to help in a variety of situations.

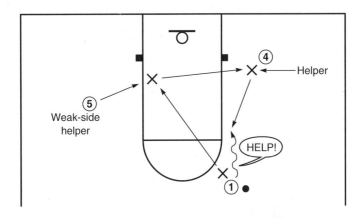

■ **Figure 8.14**   Weak-Side Help Drill.

What Is a Good Way to Scrimmage?

Full-court scrimmages with the league-standard number of players per team are fine—in fact they are essential in preparing players for games—but other practice formats have advantages. Small-sided scrimmage formats, such as 3-on-3 on the half-court, provide good learning situations. A small-sided, half-court scrimmage places more ballhandling, movement, and defensive responsibilities on each player than does the typical 5-on-5 set. And players love the quick-paced action and greater involvement of 3-on-3 competitions.

You can also organize different types of minigames, such as games in which no dribbling is permitted. These activities force players to concentrate on certain skills, such as passing and moving. The No Dribble and Pass and Move drills described next are just two scrimmage variations that promote participation and teamwork.

Scrimmage Options

Name. No Dribble (A)

Purpose. To improve passing and motion skills and get players out of the habit of dribbling needlessly on offense

Organization. Works well 5-on-5, 4-on-4, or 3-on-3 on the half-court. The offense is initiated from the top of the key, with the #1 player slapping the ball. The offense team runs its regular patterns, but the ballhandler is not allowed to dribble. If a player does dribble, the ball is turned over to the defense. If a team scores, it retains possession. If the defense rebounds a miss, it is allowed a free pass to set up on offense. If the offense rebounds a miss, it can put the ball back up or pass the ball and get back into the offensive motion. Each basket is worth 1 point; the drill is over when one team scores 5.

Coaching Points. Emphasize good passing and motion. Stop play at times if you see improper floor balance or poor screens being set. Tell players to move the ball quickly, cut sharply, and always roll to the basket.

Name. Pass and Move (A)

Purpose. To enhance offensive teamwork and shot selection, and improve team defense

Organization.   Players are 5-on-5 full-court. The offense must pass the ball at least five times before shooting, unless an uncontested layup opportunity is available. Thus, fast breaks are possible, and the defense can't just take it easy until the fourth pass. After five passes, players can continue to pass the ball as much as is necessary to get a good shot.

Coaching Points.   Emphasize motion, especially penetration, on offense. Don't let players simply pass the ball five times out front, far away from the basket. Also, watch that players choose only high-percentage shots–not merely the first thing that comes along. Encourage defensive players to maintain good position, talk when screens are set, and help out teammates who get beat. This is a very challenging drill.

How Can I Learn More About Coaching and Basketball?

Successful coaches develop only after several years of hard work, learning from their mistakes, and picking up new and effective coaching methods. Indeed, the best coaches continue to seek more information. Here are three ways you can learn more about coaching and basketball:

➡ *Keep seeking to improve your coaching.* Your players improve when they have fun, are informed, and are motivated to get better. You will too!

➡ *Attend coaching clinics.* We recommend the Coaching Principles Course that is offered throughout the country by the American Sport Education Program (ASEP).

➡ *Read up on basketball and coaching.* ASEP offers several basketball coaching resources and an excellent, general coaching resource, *Successful Coaching.*

The American Sport Education Program would be happy to help you further your coaching knowledge. For information or to order materials, contact us at

P.O. Box 5076
Champaign, IL 61825-5076
1-800-747-5698

Appendix A

Sample Season Plan for Beginning Basketball Players

Goal: To help players learn and practice the individual skills and team tactics needed to play basketball games successfully.

T(#) = Initial skill teaching time (minutes)   * = Skills practiced during drills and activities
P(#) = Review and practice time (minutes)

Skills	Week 1		Week 2		Week 3		Week 4	
	Day 1	Day 2	Day 1	Day 2	Day 1	Day 2	Day 1	Day 2
Warm-Up Exercises	T(10)	P(5)	P(5)	P(5)	P(5)	P(5)	P(5)	P(5)
Cool-Down Exercises	T(10)	P(5)	P(5)	P(5)	P(5)	P(5)	P(5)	P(5)
Passing/Catching								
Chest	T(5)	*		*	*	*	*	*
Bounce	T(5)	*		*	*	*	*	*
Overhead	T(5)	*			*	*	*	*
Drills	P(10)	P(10)		P(10)				
Dribbling								
Stationary		T(5)	*					
Walking		T(5)	*					
Running		T(5)	*		*	*		*
Drills		P(10)	P(10)					

	Week 1		Week 2		Week 3		Week 4	
Skills (*continued*)	Day 1	Day 2	Day 1	Day 2	Day 1	Day 2	Day 1	Day 2
Shooting								
Layup			T(5)	P(5)	*	*	P(5)	*
Set/Jump			T(10)	P(10)	*	*	P(5)	*
Free throw		T(5)	P(5)	*	P(5)	*	P(5)	*
Drills			P(15)	P(10)	P(10)			
Moving								
Stance				T(5)				
Stops/Pivots				(T5)	*	*	*	*
Cuts					T(5)	*	*	*
Drills					P(5)			
Rebounding				T(5)	P(5)	*	*	P(5)
Individual Defense								
On ball					T(5)	*	*	*
Off ball					T(5)	*	*	*
Drills					P(10)	P(5)		

Skills (continued)	Week 1		Week 2		Week 3		Week 4	
	Day 1	Day 2	Day 1	Day 2	Day 1	Day 2	Day 1	Day 2
Offensive Team Play								
Court balance						T(5)	*	*
Motion						T(5)	*	*
Screens						T(5)	P(5)	*
Inbounds							T(5)	P(5)
Fast break							T(5)	P(10)
3-on-3 half-court						P(10)		P(10)
5-on-5 full-court						P(10)		P(10)
Drills							P(10)	
Defensive Team Play								
Position			T(5)		*	*	*	*
Help						T(5)	*	*
Screens						T(5)	*	*
Drills							P(10)	P(10)
Elapsed time	45	50	60	60	60	60	60	60

Appendix B

Official Basketball Signals

Start clock

Stop clock
for jump ball

Beckon substitute
when ball is dead
and clock stopped

Stop clock
for foul

Point(s) scored
(1 or 2)

Blocking

Over-and-back or
carrying the ball

Bonus situation (for second
throw drop one arm)

Pushing

Illegal use of
hands

Technical
foul

3-second violation

Designates out of bounds spot
and direction ball will go

Traveling (follow with direction signal)

Holding

No score (follow with direction signal)

Illegal dribble

Appendix C

Organizations to Contact for Coaching Children With Disabilities

American Athletic Association of the Deaf
3607 Washington Boulevard, Suite 4
Ogden, UT 84403-1737
(801) 393-8710
TTY: (801) 393-7916
Fax: (801) 393-2263

Disabled Sports USA
451 Hungerford Drive, Suite 100
Rockville, MD 20850
(301) 217-0960

Paralyzed Veterans of America
801 18th Street NW
Washington, DC 20006
(202) 872-1300
(800) 424-8200

Special Olympics International
1325 G Street NW, Suite 500
Washington, DC 20005
(202) 628-3630

U.S. Association of Blind Athletes
33 North Institute
Colorado Springs, CO 80903
(719) 630-0422

U.S. Cerebral Palsy Athletic Association
3810 West NW Highway, Suite 205
Dallas, TX 75220
(214) 351-1510

U.S. Les Autres Sports Association
1475 West Gray, Suite166
Houston, TX 77019-4926
(713) 521-3737

Basketball resources for coaches and players

Hal Wissel

1994 • Paper • 224 pp
Item PWIS0691 • ISBN 0-87322-691-7
$14.95 ($20.95 Canadian)

"Basketball: Steps to Success has the innovative instruction and drills you need to master the fundamentals that will improve your total game."
> Dean Smith
> Head Basketball Coach
> University of North Carolina

Jerry Krause, EdD

Foreword by Dean Smith
1991 • Paper • 136 pp
Item PKRA0422 • ISBN 0-88011-422-3
$16.95 ($23.95 Canadian)

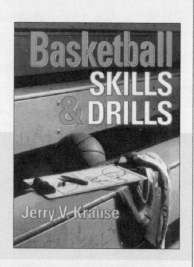

"A masterful job of writing a book that will help both players and coaches recognize and reach their full potential. I recommend this book to every person who has or will lace up a shoe to play or blow a whistle to coach."
> Jud Heathcote
> Former Head Basketball Coach
> Michigan State University

To place your order, U.S. customers
call TOLL FREE 1 800 747-4457.
Customers outside the U.S. place your order using
the appropriate telephone number/address
shown in the front of this book.

    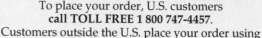

Human Kinetics
The Premier Publisher for Sports & Fitness

2335

Prices subject to change.

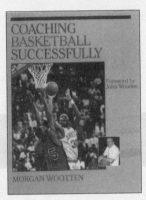
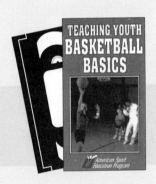

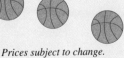

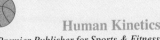